BRADLEY'S NEW GIANT PIANO BOOK

arranged by RICHARD BRADLEY

Richard Bradley is one of the world's best-known and best-selling arrangers of piano music for print. His success can be attributed to years of experience as a teacher and his understanding of students' and players' needs. His innovative piano methods for adults (Bradley's How to Play Piano—Adult Books 1, 2, and 3) and kids (Bradley for Kids—Red, Blue, and Green Series) not only teach the instrument, but they also teach musicianship each step of the way.

Originally from the Chicago area, Richard completed his undergraduate and graduate work at the Chicago Conservatory of Music and Roosevelt University. After college, Richard became a print arranger for Hansen Publications and later became music director of Columbia Pictures Publications. In 1977, he co-founded his own publishing company, Bradley Publications, which is now exclusively distributed worldwide by Warner Bros. Publications.

Richard is equally well known for his piano workshops, clinics, and teacher training seminars. He was a panelist for the first and second Keyboard Teachers' National Video Conferences, which were attended by more than 20,000 piano teachers throughout the United States.

The home video version of his adult teaching method, *How to Play Piano With Richard Bradley,* was nominated for an American Video Award as Best Music Instruction Video, and, with sales climbing each year since its release, it has brought thousands of adults to—or back to—piano lessons. Still, Richard advises, "The video can only get an adult started and show them what they can do. As they advance, all students need direct input from an accomplished teacher."

Additional Richard Bradley videos aimed at other than the beginning pianist include *How to Play Blues Piano* and *How to Play Jazz Piano.* As a frequent television talk show guest on the subject of music education, Richard's many appearances include "Hour Magazine" with Gary Collins, "The Today Show," and "Mother's Day" with former "Good Morning America" host Joan Lunden, as well as dozens of local shows.

Project Manager: ZOBEIDA PÉREZ
Art Design: OLIVIA DARVAS NOVAK

BRADLEY™ is a trademark of Warner Bros. Publications

© 2003 BRADLEY PUBLICATIONS
All Rights Assigned to and Controlled by WARNER BROS. PUBLICATIONS U.S. INC.,
15800 N.W. 48th Avenue, Miami, FL 33014

ALPHABETICAL CONTENTS

CONTENTS BY CATEGORY

CLASSICS

PATRIOTIC SONGS

STANDARDS

THE GAME OF LOVE

Recorded by Santana featuring Michelle Branch

Words and Music by
ALEX ANDER and RICHARD W. NOWELS, JR.
Arranged by Richard Bradley

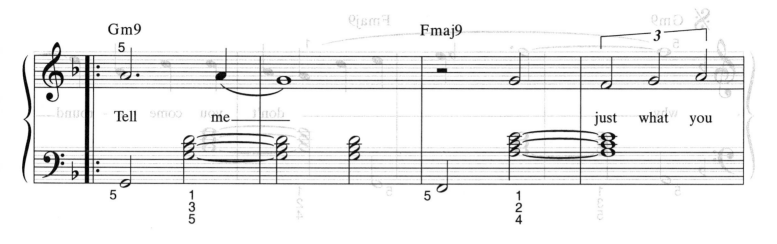

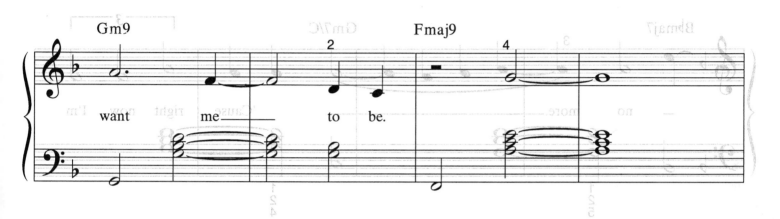

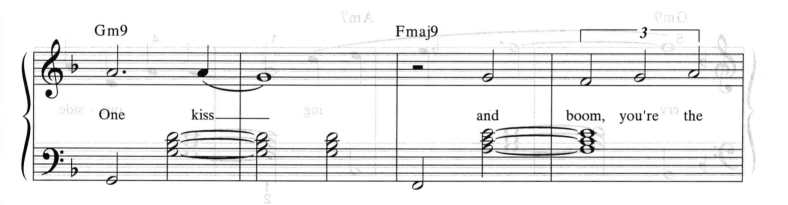

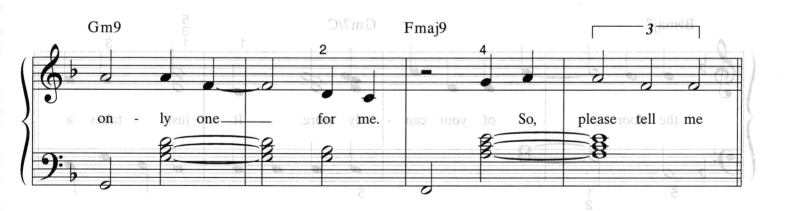

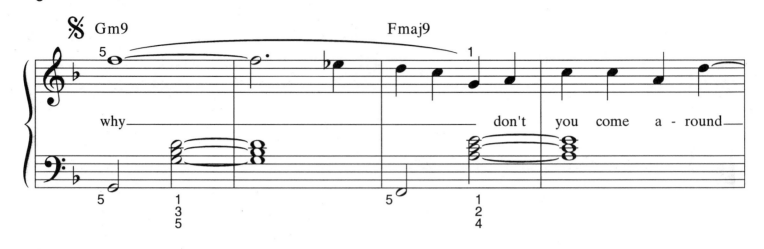

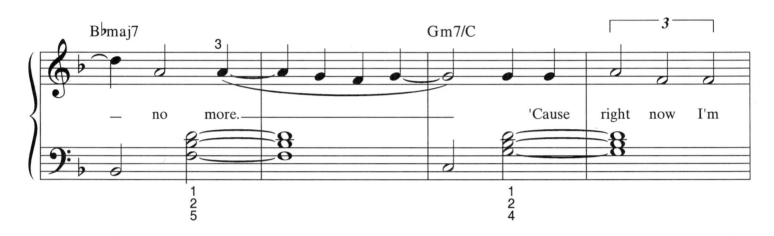

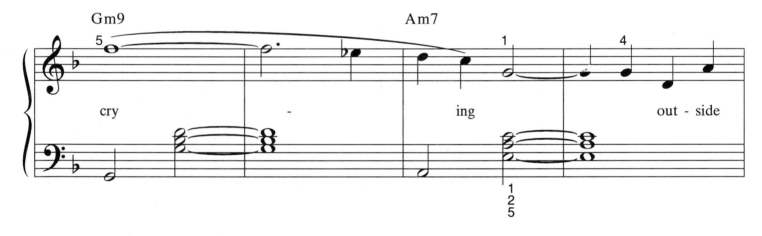

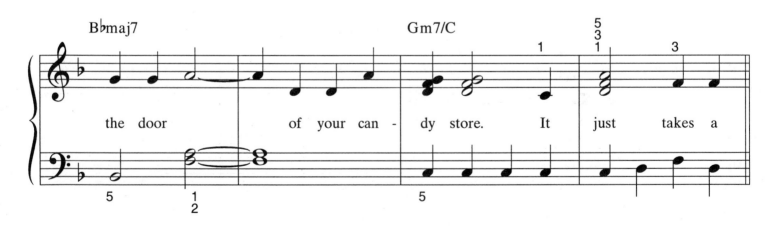

Chorus:

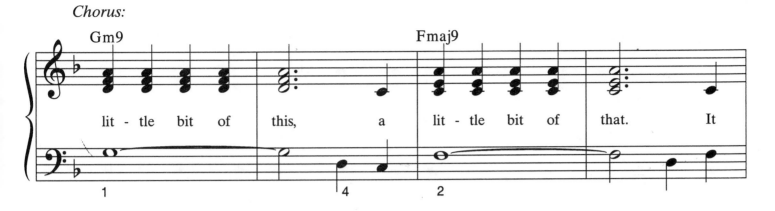

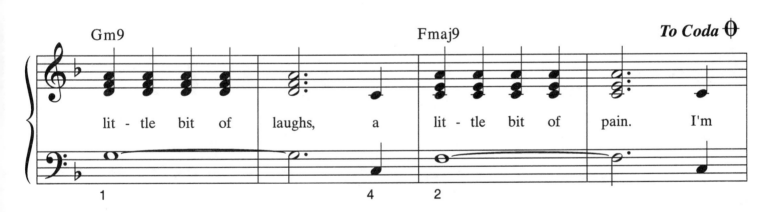

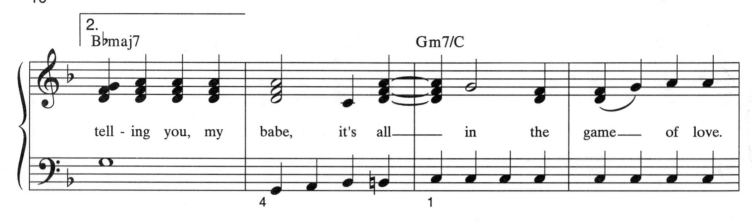

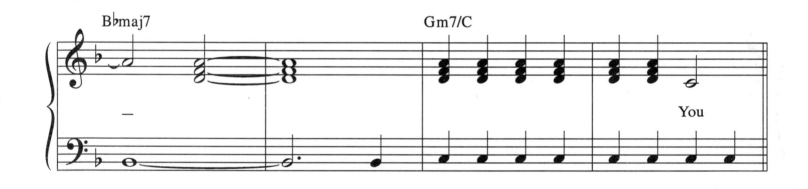

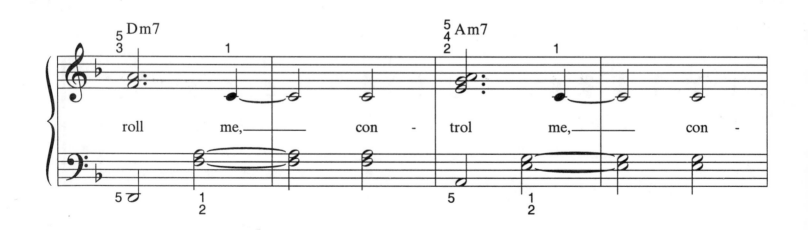

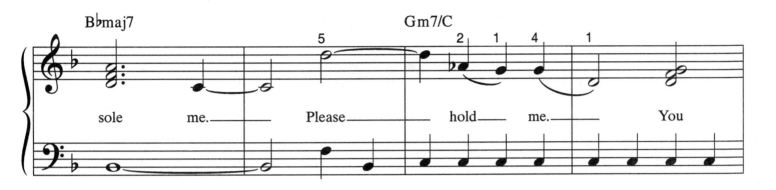

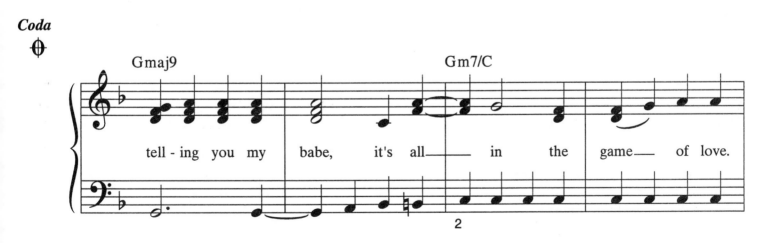

12

Gm9   Fmaj9

It's all — in the game — of love.

Gm9   Fmaj9

It's all — in the game of love.

Gm9   Fmaj9

Let's play the game of love.

B♭maj7   Gm7/C   *Repeat and fade*

Verse 2:
This, whatever you make it to be,
Sunshine set on the cold, lonely sea.
So please, baby,
Try and use me for what I'm good for.
It ain't saying goodbye,
It's knocking down the door
Of your candy store.
It just takes a . . .
(To Chorus:)

Verse 3:
So, please tell me
Why don't you come around no more.
'Cause right now I'm dying
Outside the door of your loving store
It just takes a . . .
(To Chorus:)

A THOUSAND MILES

Recorded by Vanessa Carlton

Words and Music by
VANESSA CARLTON
Arranged by Richard Bradley

to - night.

don't want to   let   you___   know

Verse 2:
It's always times like these when I think of you
And wonder if you ever think of me.
'Cause everything's so wrong and I don't belong
Livin' in your precious memory.
'Cause I need you,
And I miss you,
And I wonder . . .
(To Chorus:)

FOREVER AND FOR ALWAYS

Recorded by Shania Twain

Words and Music by
SHANIA TWAIN and R. J. LANGE
Arranged by Richard Bradley

1st and 3rd time instrumental

2. I can

hear your heart___ beat now.___

I can

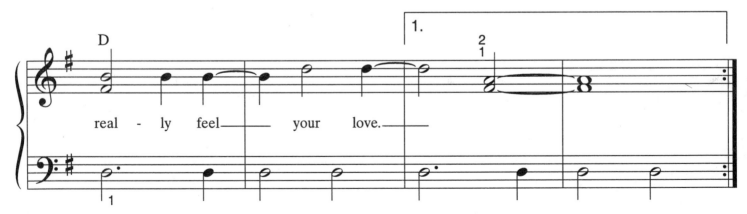

real - ly feel___ your love.___

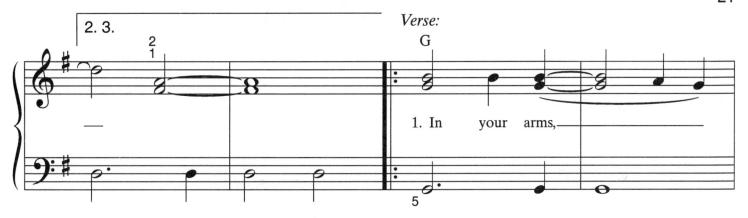

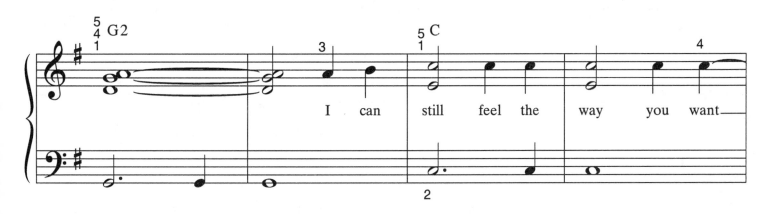

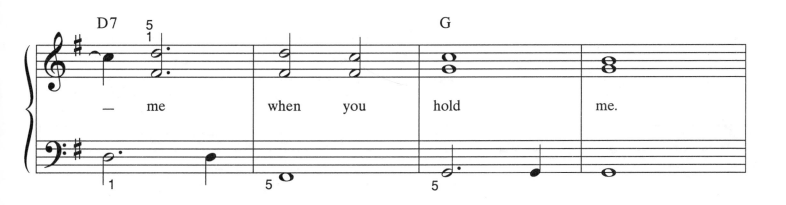

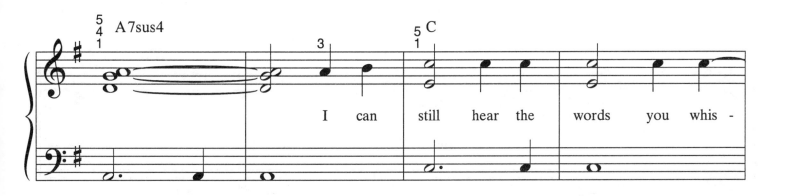

24

Coda

I'm keep - ing you_____ for - ev -

er and_____ for al - ways.

We will be_____ to - geth - er all_____

_____ of our days. Wan - na

wake up ev - 'ry morn - ing to your

I'm

in   your   arms.

Verse 2:
In your heart,
I can still hear a beat
For everytime you kiss me.
And when we're apart,
I know how much you miss me,
I can feel your love
For me in your heart.

And there ain't no way
I'm letting you go now.
And there ain't no way
And there ain't no how,
I'll never see that day.
(To Chorus:)

Verse 3:
In your eyes,
I can still see the look
Of the one who really loves me.
The one who wouldn't put anything else
In the world above me.
I can still see the love
For me in your eyes.

And there aint no way
I'm letting you go now.
And there ain't no way
And there ain't no how,
I'll never see that day.
(To Chorus:)

THIS IS THE NIGHT

Recorded by Clay Aiken

Words and Music by
CHRISTOPHER BRAIDE,
GARY BURR and ALDO NOVA
Arranged by Richard Bradley

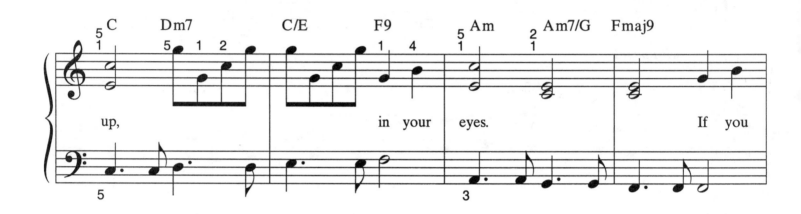

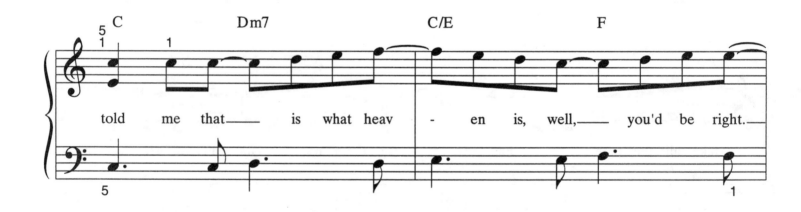

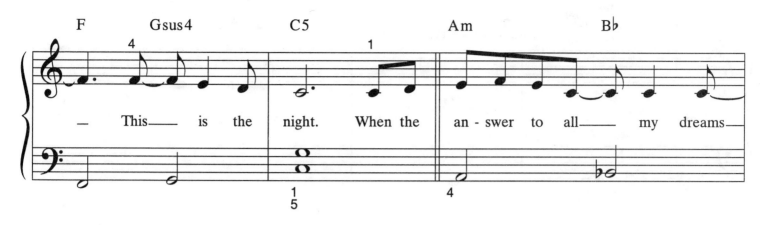

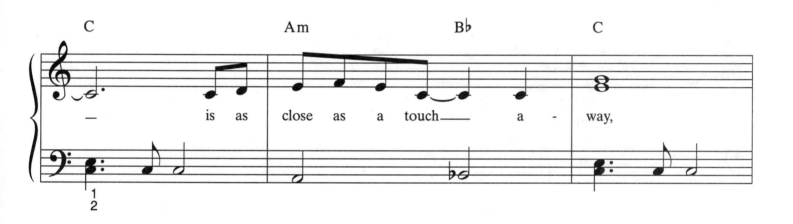

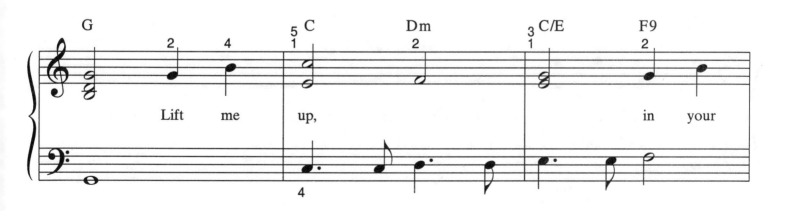

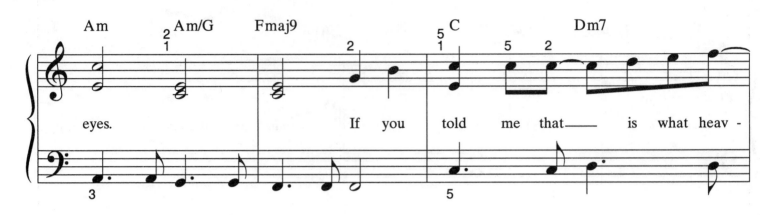

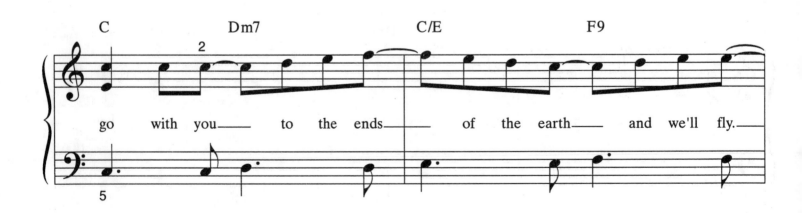

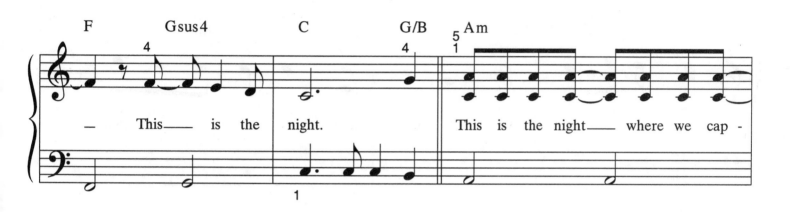

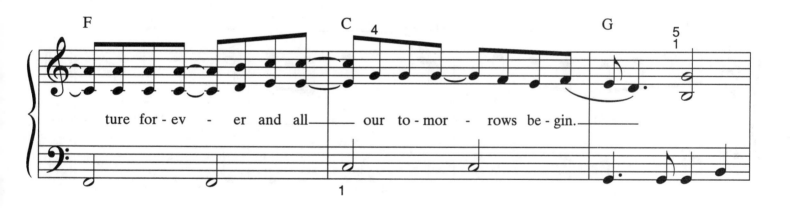

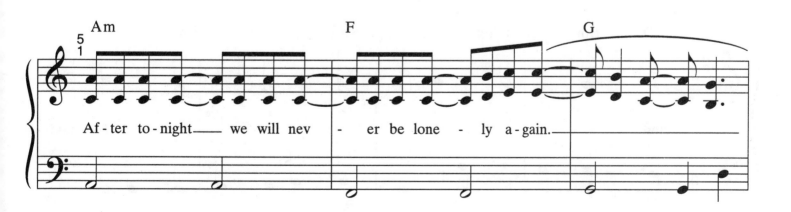

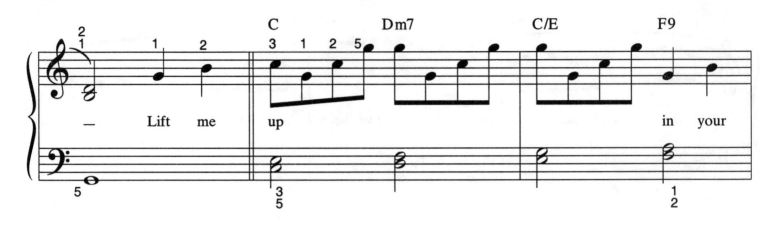

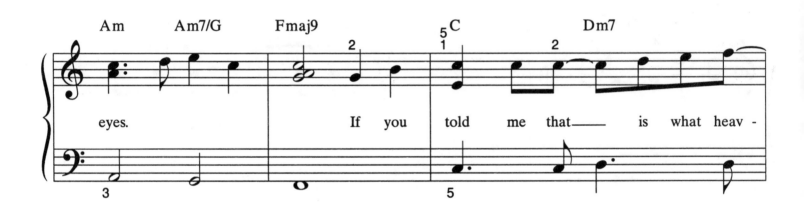

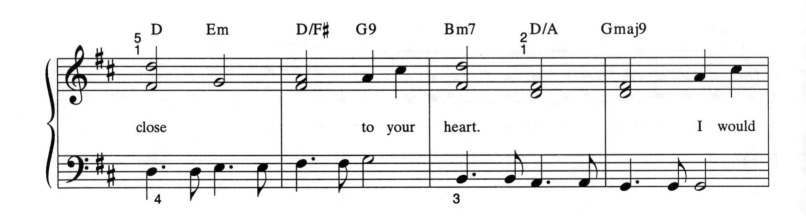

go   with   you____   to   the   ends____   of   the   earth____   and   we'll   fly.

I've   been

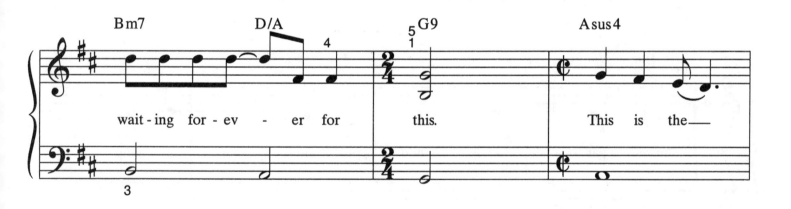

wait - ing   for - ev - er   for   this.   This   is   the__

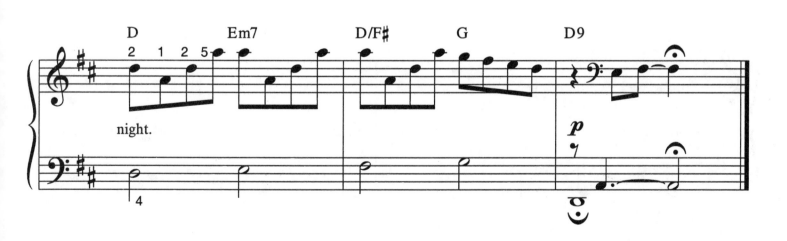

night.

BIG YELLOW TAXI

Recorded by Counting Crows featuring Vanessa Carlton

Words and Music by
JONI MITCHELL
Arranged by Richard Bradley

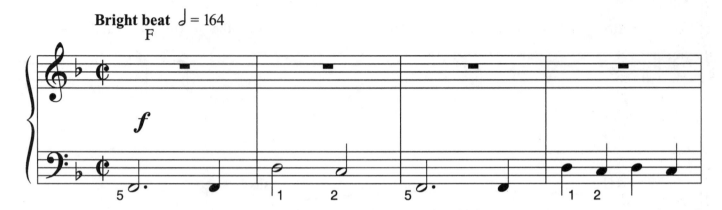

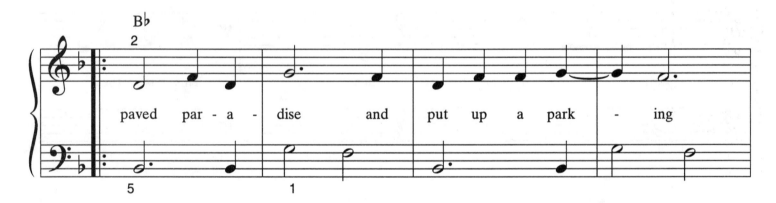

Big Yellow Taxi - 4 - 1

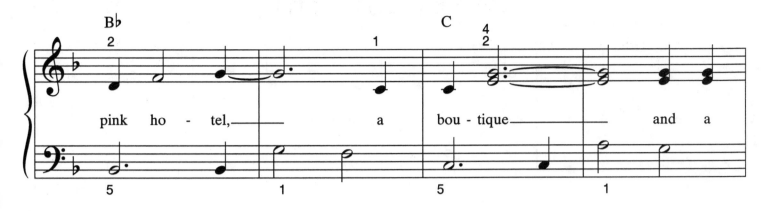

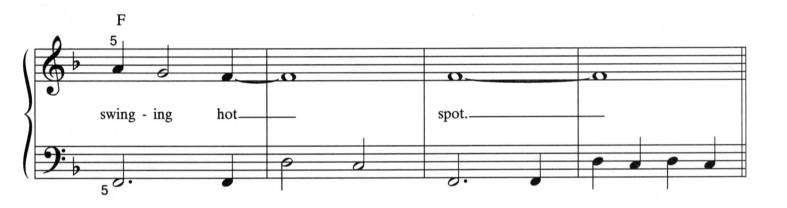

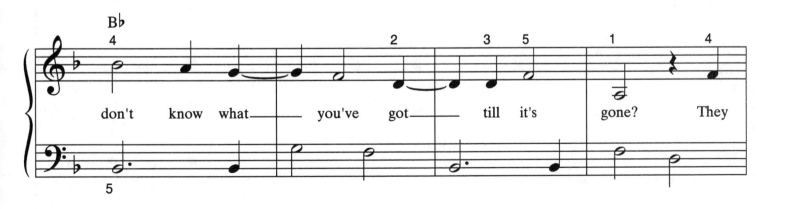

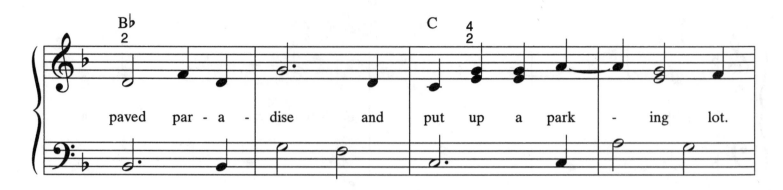

paved par - a - dise and put up a park - ing lot.

1. 2. 3.

Woo,_____ pa,__ pa, pa,__ pa.

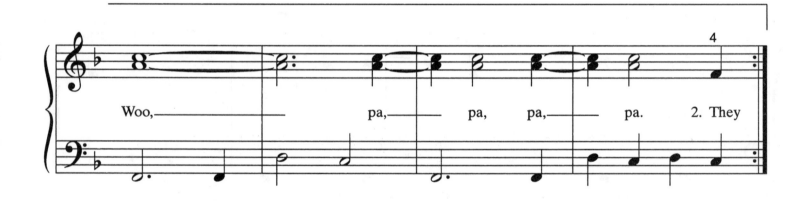

Woo,_____ pa,__ pa, pa,__ pa. 2. They

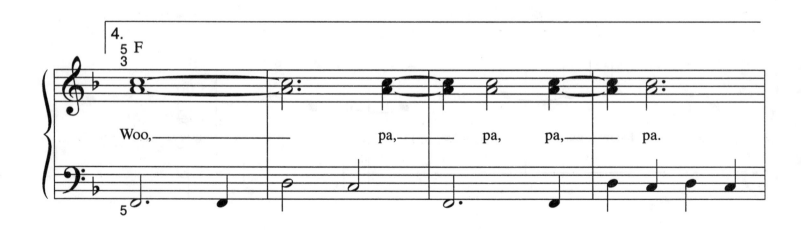

4.

Woo,_____ pa,__ pa, pa,__ pa.

Verse 2:
They took all the trees
And put them in a tree museum,
And they charged all the people
A dollar and a half just to see them.
(To Chorus:)

Verse 3:
Hey, farmer, farmer,
Put away that D.D.T. now,
Give me spots on my apples
But leave me the birds and the bees,
Please!
(To Chorus)

Verse 4:
Late, late last night
I heard the screen door slam,
And a big yellow taxi
Took away my old man.
(To Chorus:)

SOAK UP THE SUN

Recorded by Sheryl Crow

Words and Music by
SHERYL CROW and JEFF TROTT
Arranged by Richard Bradley

Soak Up the Sun - 6 - 1

Chorus:

I'm _____ gon - na soak up the sun, _____

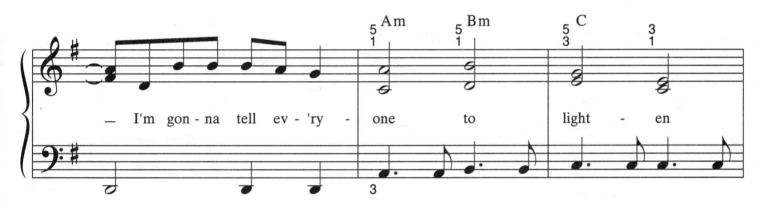

— I'm gon - na tell ev - 'ry - one to light - en

up. _____ I'm gon - na tell 'em that I've _____

CAN'T GET YOU OUT OF MY HEAD

Recorded by Kylie Minogue

Words and Music by
ROBERT DAVIS and CATHY DENNIS
Arranged by Richard Bradley

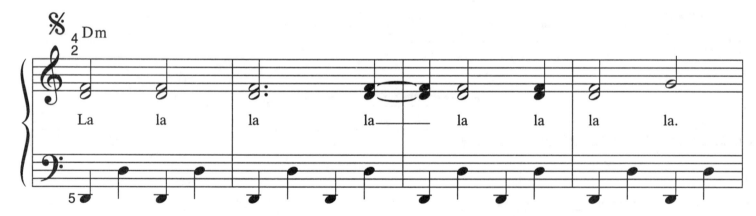

La   la   la   la——   la   la   la   la.

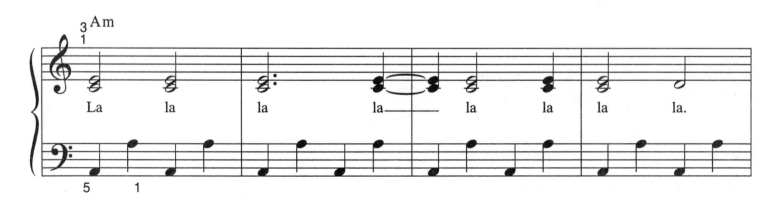

La   la   la   la——   la   la   la   la.

Can't Get You Out of My Head - 6 - 1

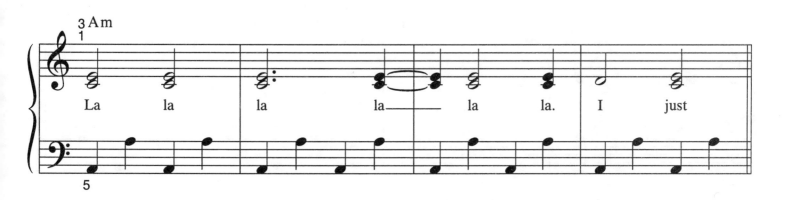

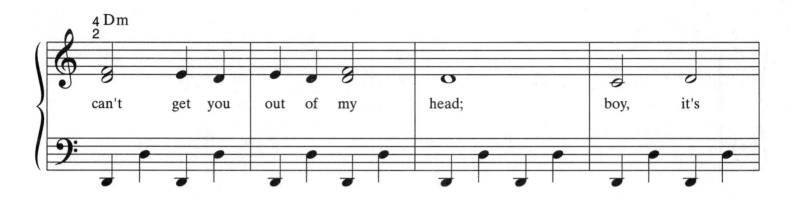

can't   get you   out of my   head;   boy,   it's

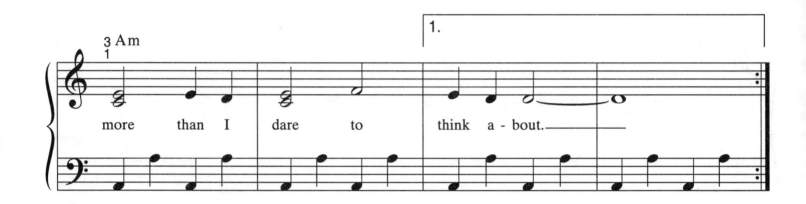

1.

more   than I   dare to   think a - bout.___

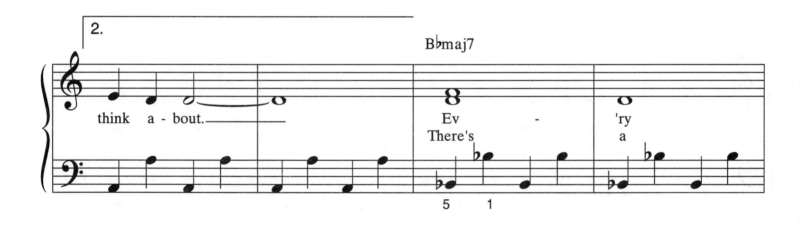

2.   B♭maj7

think a - bout.___   Ev -   'ry
                          There's   a

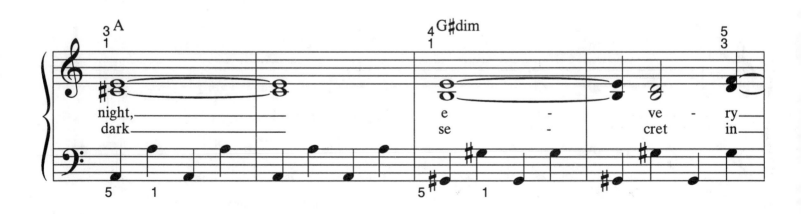

A   G♯dim

night,___   e -   ve - ry
dark___   se -   cret in

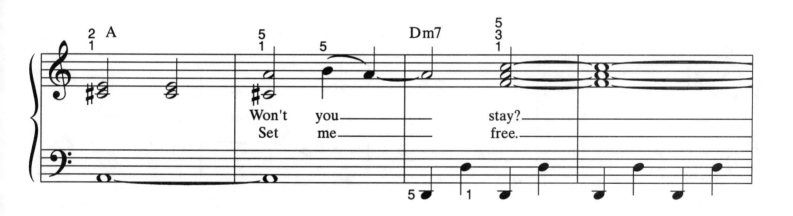

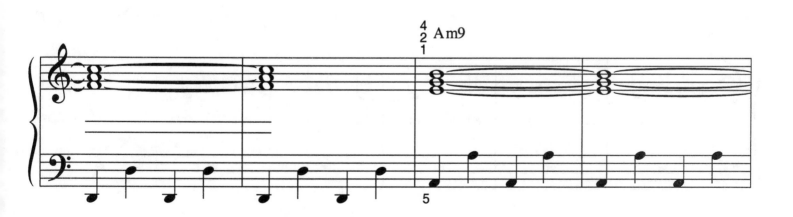

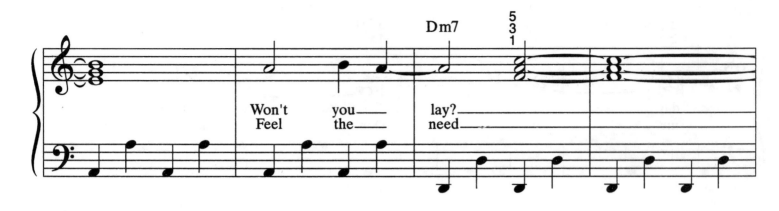

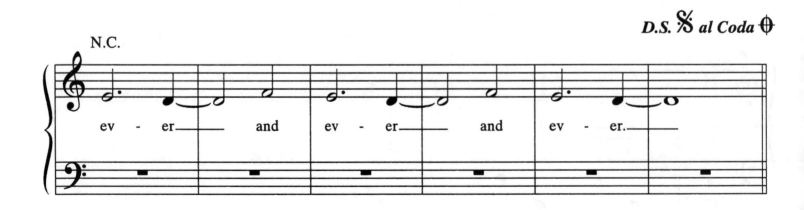

Coda

me._____ Set me free.__

Stay_____ for

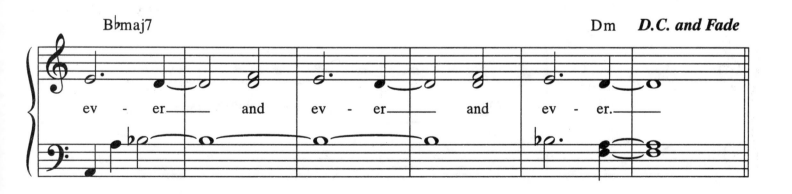

ev- er____ and ev- er____ and ev- er.

I'M LIKE A BIRD

Recorded by Nelly Furtado

Words and Music by
NELLY FURTADO
Arranged by Richard Bradley

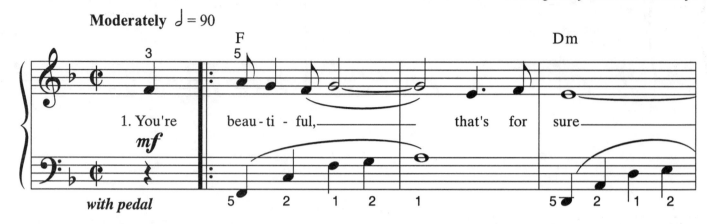

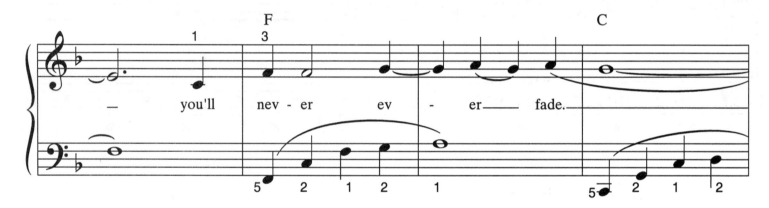

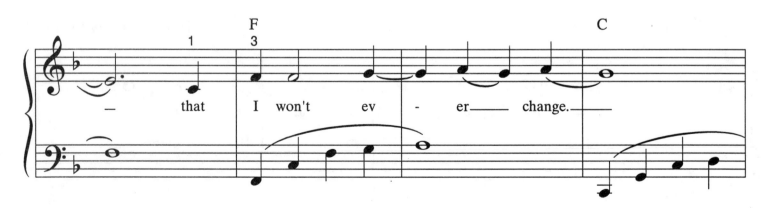

I'm Like a Bird - 6 - 1

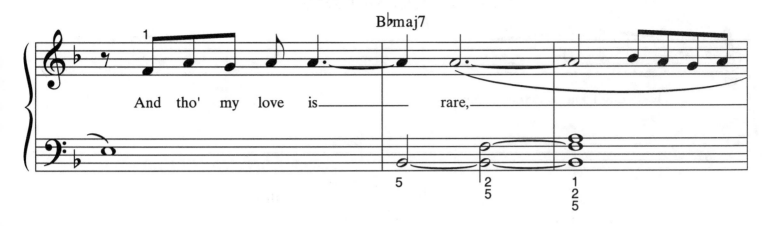

And tho' my love is ___ rare,

C

yeah, ___ and tho' my love is true. ___

B♭maj7

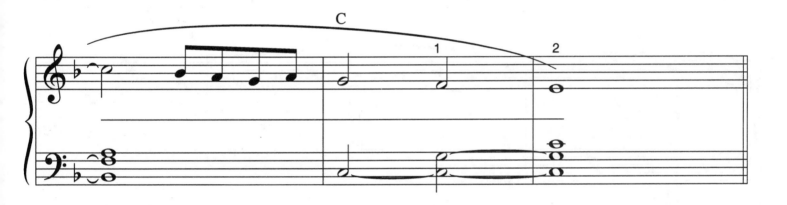

C

Chorus:

F   C/E

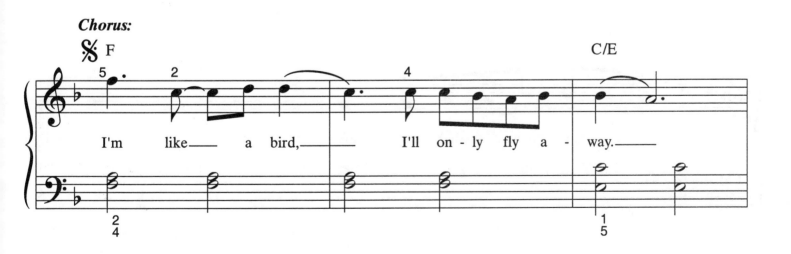

I'm like ___ a bird, ___ I'll on-ly fly a-way. ___

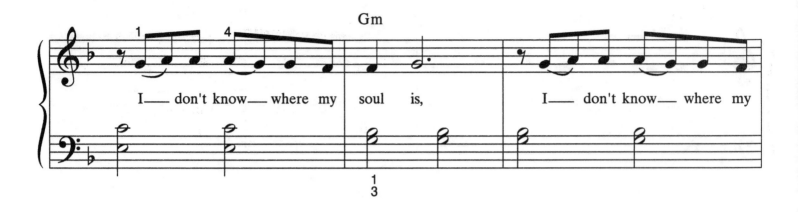

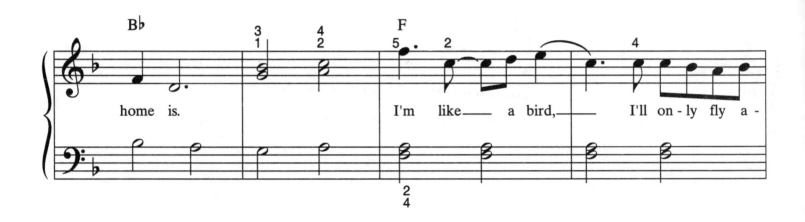

home is.

It's not that I wan - na say good -

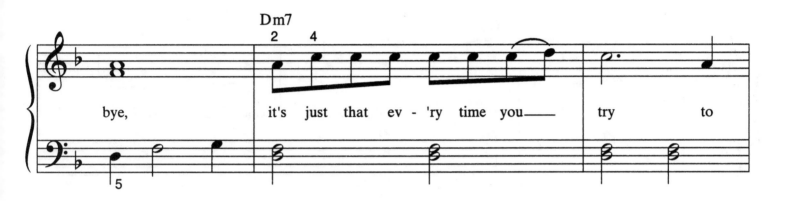

bye,

it's just that ev - 'ry time you___ try to

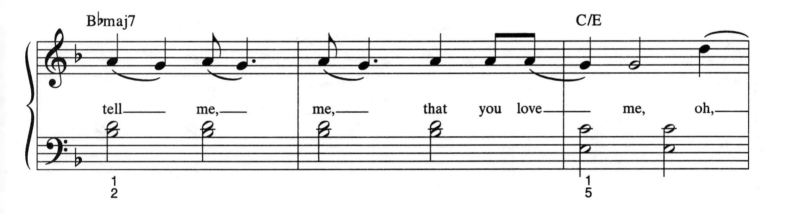

tell___ me,___ me,___ that you love___ me, oh,

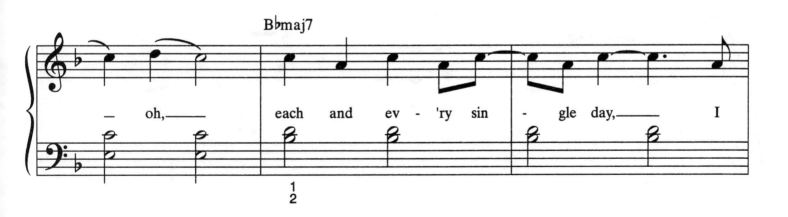

___ oh,___ each and ev - 'ry sin - gle day,___ I

Verse 2:
Your faith in me brings me to tears
Even after all these years.
And it pains me so much
To tell that you don't know me that well.
And tho' my love is rare, yeah,
And tho' my love is true.
(To Chorus:)

DANCE WITH MY FATHER

Recorded by Luther Vandross

Words and Music by
LUTHER VANDROSS
and RICHARD MARX
Arranged by Richard Bradley

all the in - no - cence, my fa - ther would

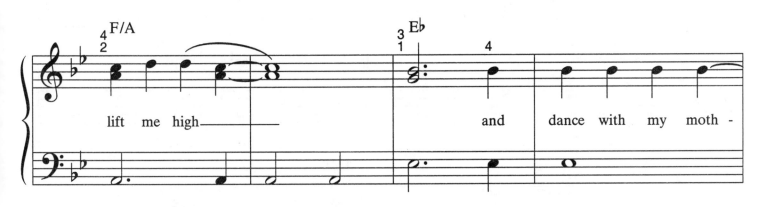

lift me high and dance with my moth -

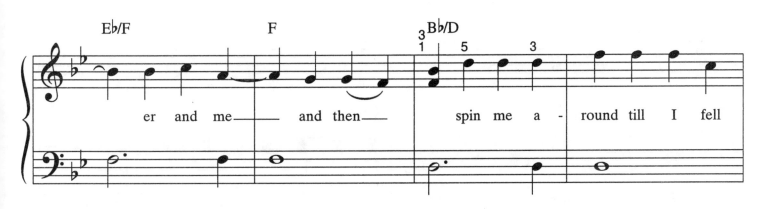

er and me and then spin me a - round till I fell

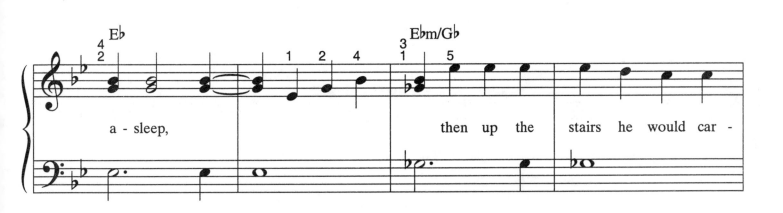

a - sleep, then up the stairs he would car -

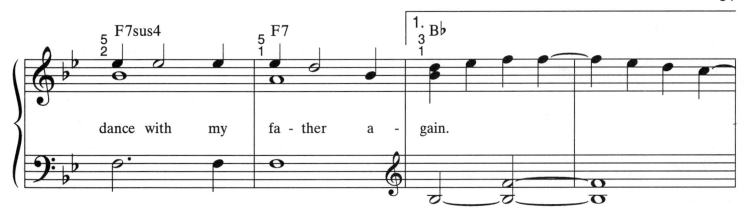

dance with my fa - ther a - gain.

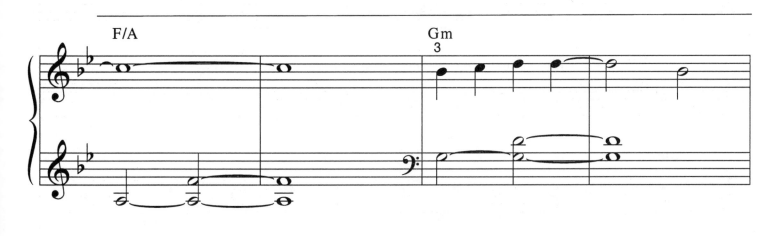

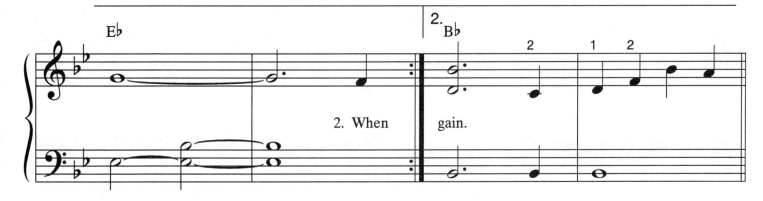

2. When gain.

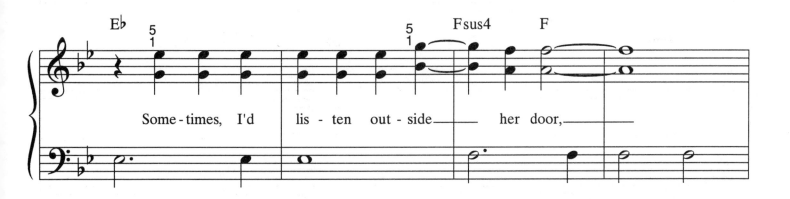

Some - times, I'd lis - ten out - side her door,

Verse 2:

When I and my mother would disagree,
To get my way, I would run from her to him.
He'd make me laugh just to comfort me,
Then finally, make me do just what my mother said.
Later at night, when I was asleep,
He'd left a dollar under my sheet.

Never dreamed that he would be gone from me.
If I could steal one final glance, one final step,
One final dance with him.
I'd play a song that would never end.
'Cause I'd love, love, love
To dance with my father again.

I HOPE YOU DANCE

Recorded by Lee Ann Womack with Sons of the Desert

Words and Music by
MARK D. SANDERS
and TIA SILLERS
Arranged by Richard Bradley

Verse:

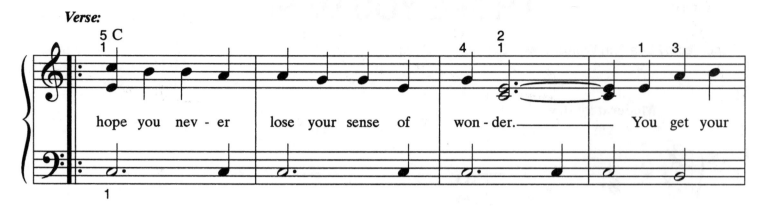

hope you nev - er   lose your sense of   won - der._____   You get your

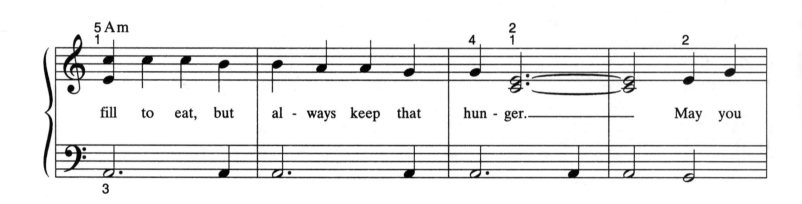

fill   to   eat, but   al - ways keep that   hun - ger._____   May you

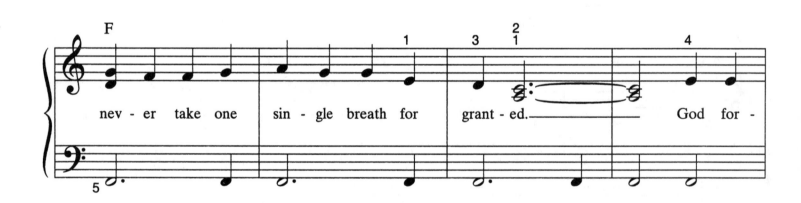

nev - er take one   sin - gle breath for   grant - ed._____   God for -

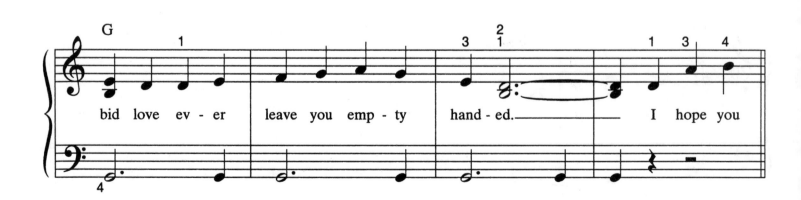

bid love ev - er   leave you emp - ty   hand - ed._____   I hope you

Chorus:

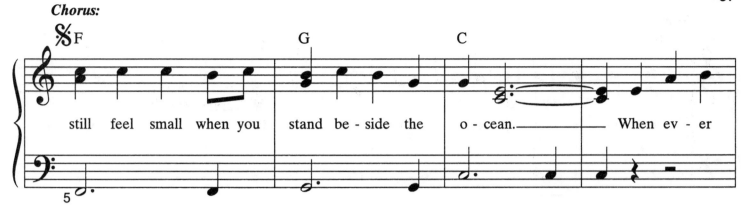

still feel small when you | stand be - side the | o - cean._____ | When ev - er

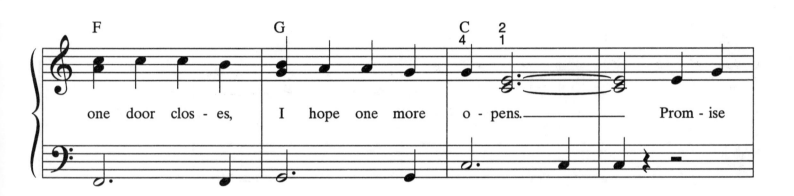

one door clos - es, | I hope one more | o - pens._____ | Prom - ise

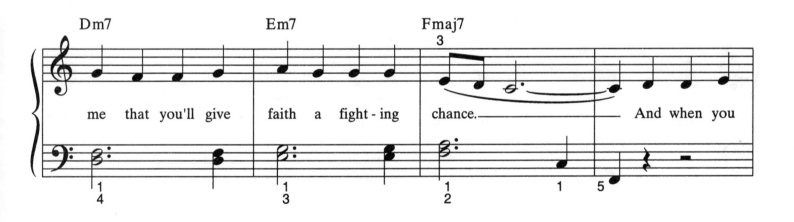

me that you'll give | faith a fight - ing | chance._____ | And when you

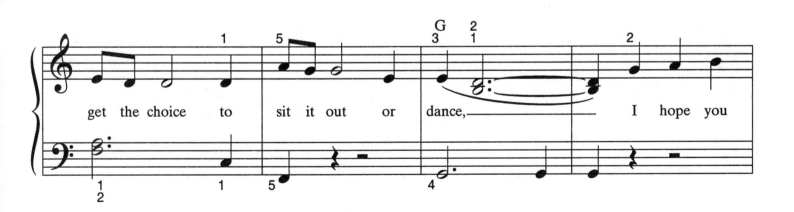

get the choice to | sit it out or | dance,_____ | I hope you

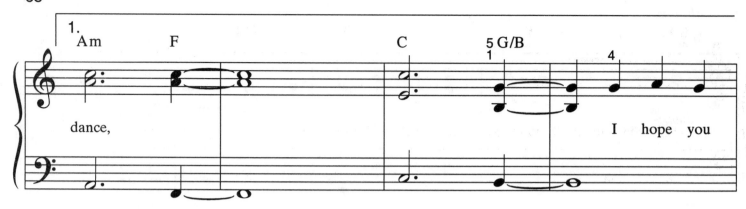

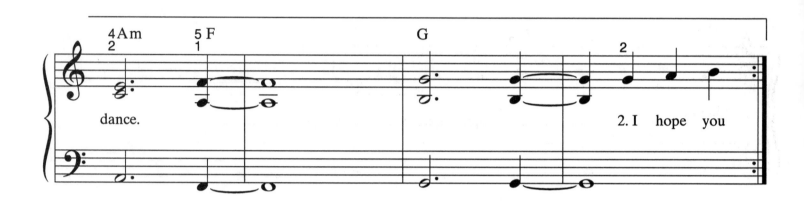

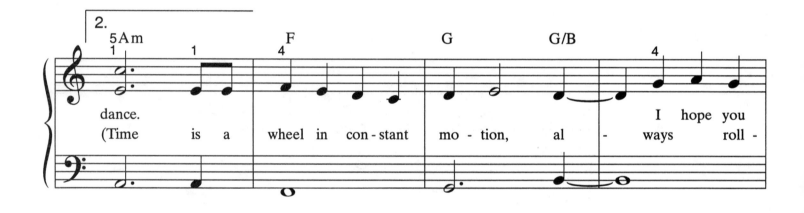

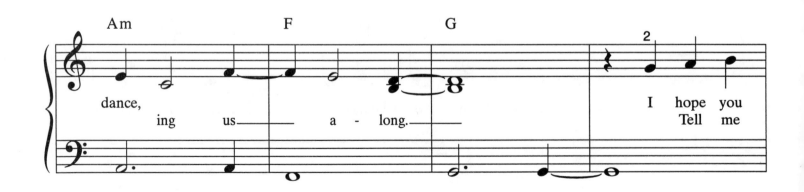

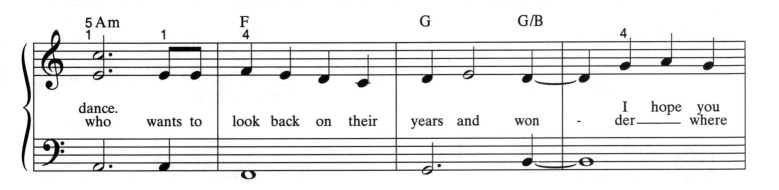

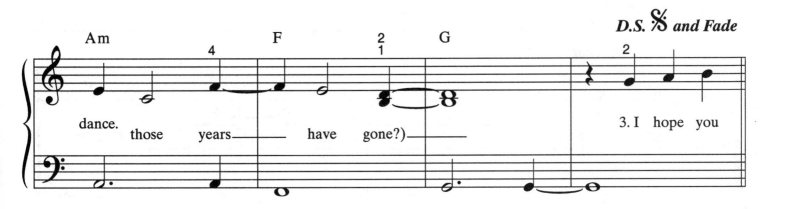

Verse 2:

I hope you never fear those mountains in the distance,
Never settle for the path of least resistance.
Livin' might mean takin' chances but they're worth takin'.
Lovin' might be a mistake but it's worth makin'.

Chorus 2:

Don't let some hell-bent heart leave you bitter.
When you come close to sellin' out, reconsider.
Give the heavens above more than just a passing glance,
And when you get the chance to sit it out or dance,...

THIS I PROMISE YOU

Recorded by ★NSYNC

Words and Music by
RICHARD MARX
Arranged by Richard Bradley

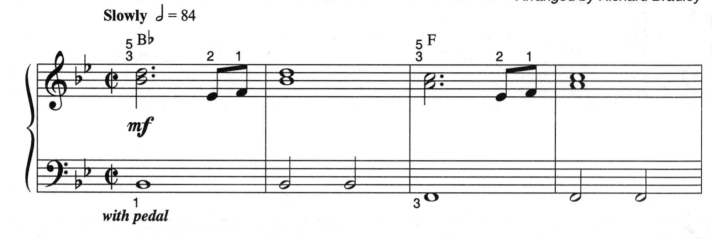

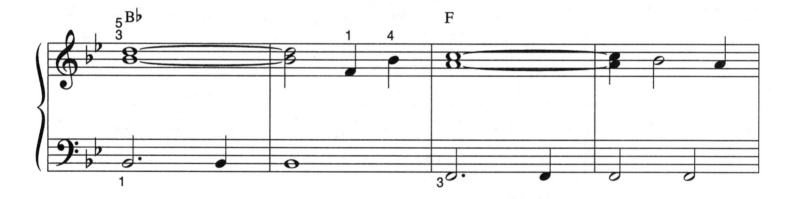

This I Promise You - 6 - 1

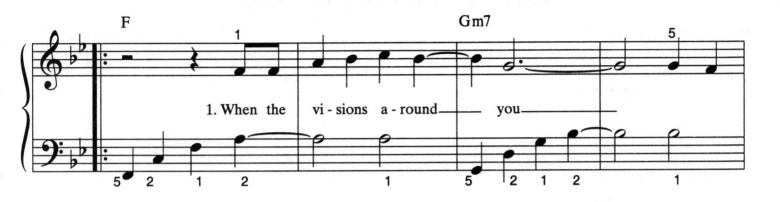

1. When the vi - sions a - round you

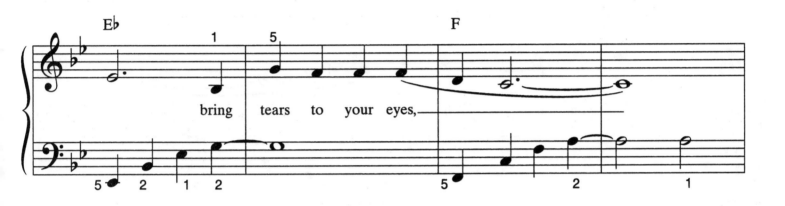

bring tears to your eyes,

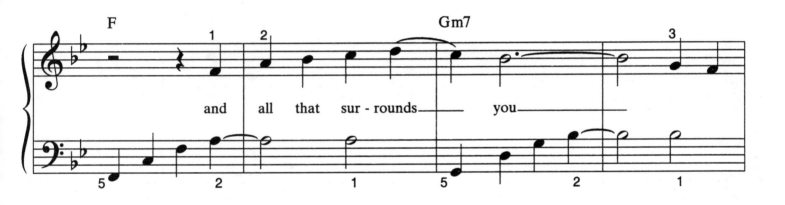

and all that sur - rounds you

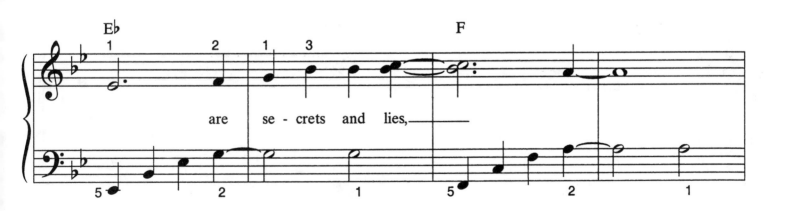

are se - crets and lies,

72

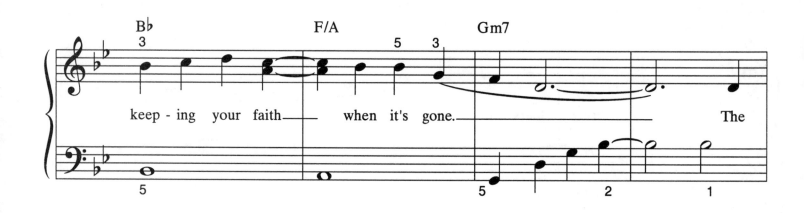

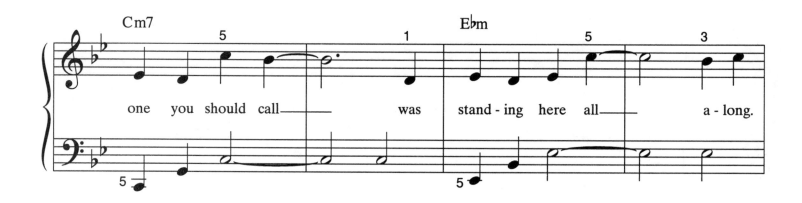

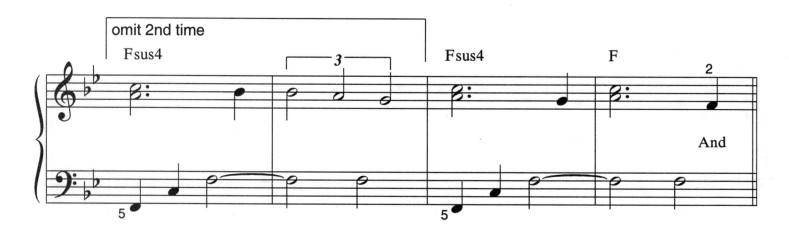

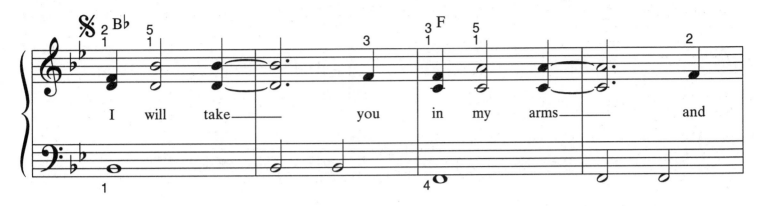

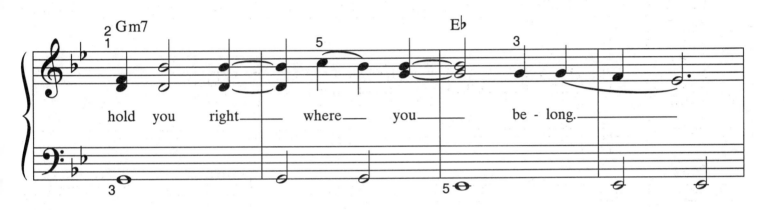

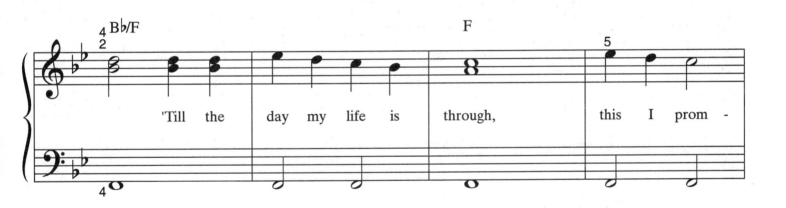

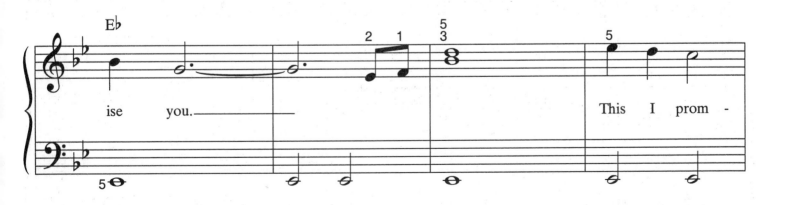

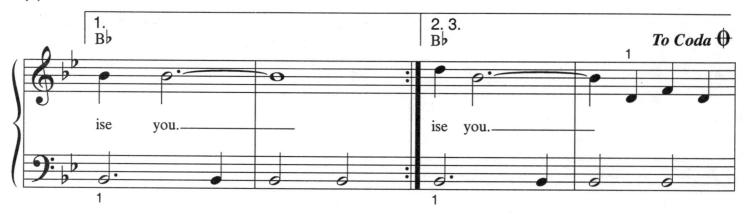

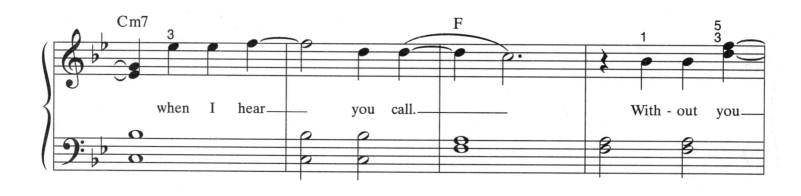

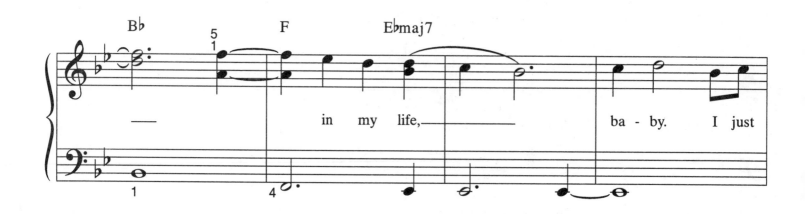

Coda

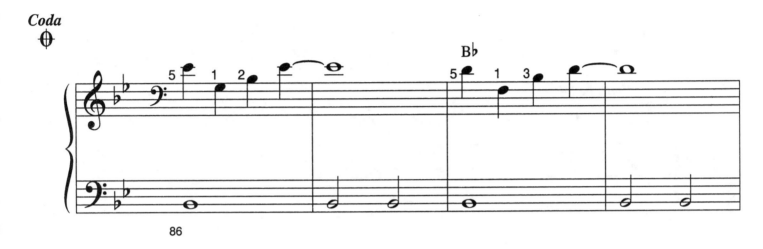

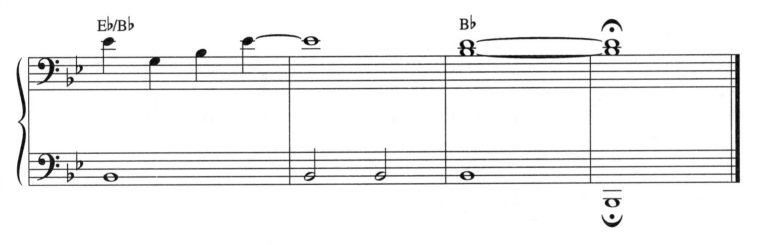

Verse 2:
I've loved you forever in lifetimes before.
And I promise you, never will you hurt anymore.
I give you my word. I give you my heart.
This is the battle I've won.
And with this vow, forever has now begun.
Just close your eyes each loving day
And know this feeling won't go away.

1st time : 'Till the day my life is through,
This I promise you, this I promise you.

2nd time : Every word I say is true,
This I promise you. Ooh, I promise you.

SHAPE OF MY HEART

Recorded by Backstreet Boys

Words and Music by
MAX MARTIN, RAMI
and LISA MISKOVSKY
Arranged by Richard Bradley

1. Ba - by, please try to for - give me.

Stay here, don't put out the glow.

Hold me now, don't both -

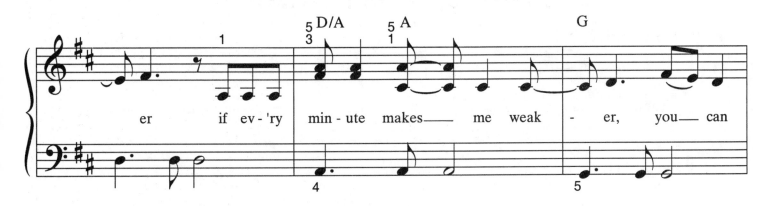

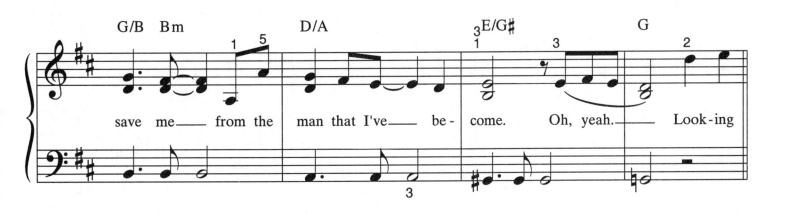

Chorus:

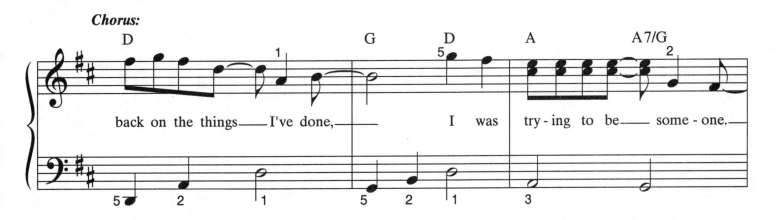

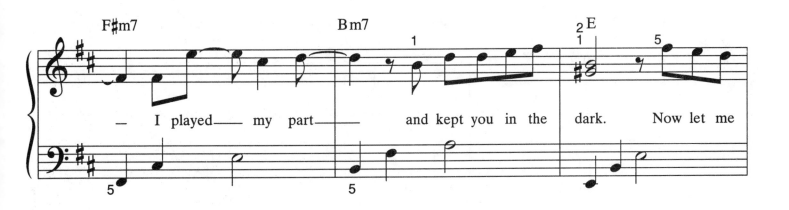

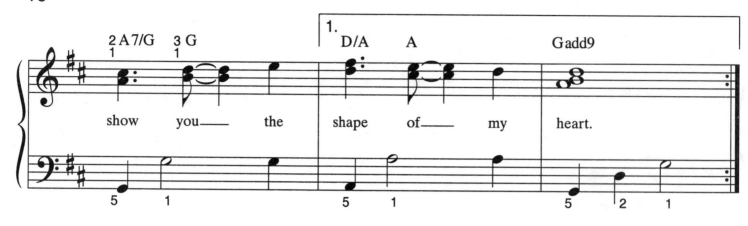

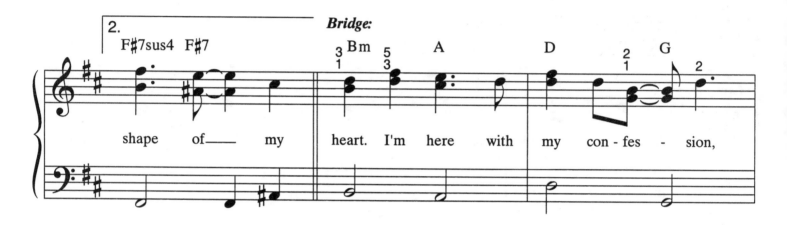

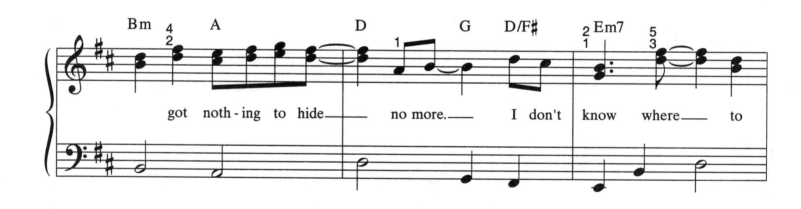

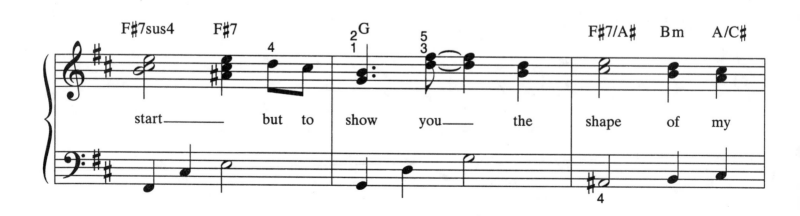

78

Verse 2:
Sadness is beautiful.
Loneliness is tragical.
So help me, I can't win this war.
Touch me now,
Don't bother if every second makes me weaker,
You can save me from the man that I've become.
Oh, yeah. Looking. . .
(To Chorus)

WHAT THE WORLD NEEDS

Recorded by Wynonna

Words and Music by
HOLLY LAMAR and BRETT JAMES
Arranged by Richard Bradley

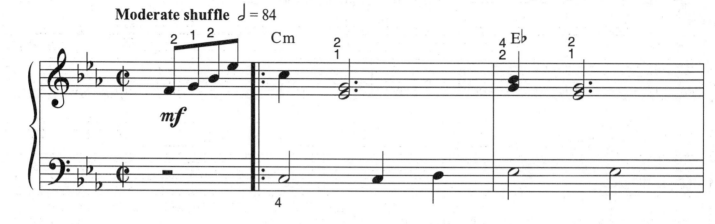

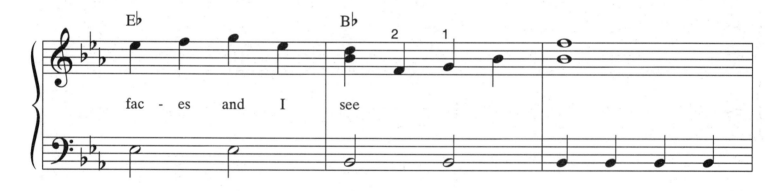

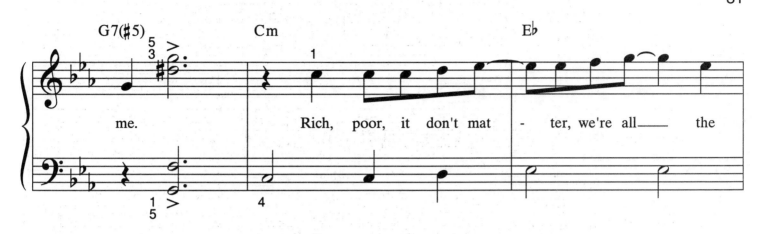

me. Rich, poor, it don't mat - ter, we're all_____ the

same. Ev-'ry-bod-y's hun-gry in a dif-f'rent way._____ We're claw-ing and

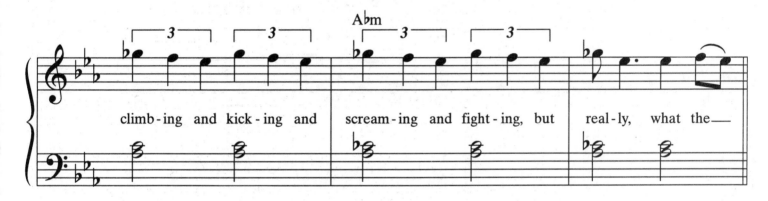

climb-ing and kick-ing and scream-ing and fight-ing, but real-ly, what the_____

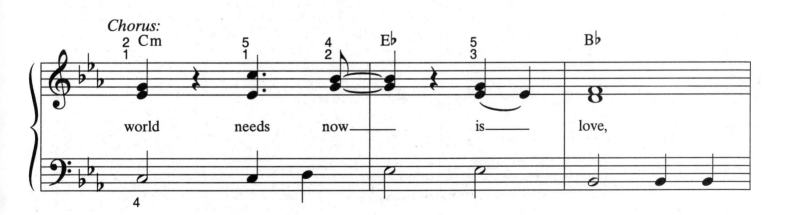

Chorus:

world needs now_____ is_____ love,

love and on - ly love.___ A lit - tle___ help___ from up a - bove;

___ fit to make___ a bet - ter day. Lets come to -

geth - er, lay___ our dif - fer - ence - es down.___

Spread it all___ a - round,___ that's what the___

world   needs———   now.———

that's   what   the———   world   needs———   now.

Verse 2:
Sometimes all it takes is just a smile
To change somebody's weather;
Chase the clouds out of their sky.
Sometimes you got to give and not receive.
Sometime you got to live what you believe.
Open your arms, 'cause that's where it starts,
Right here with you and with me.
(To Chorus:)

HERO

Recorded by Enrique Iglesias

Words and Music by
ENRIQUE IGLESIAS,
PAUL BARRY and MARK TAYLOR
Arranged by Richard Bradley

Moderately slow ♩ = 82

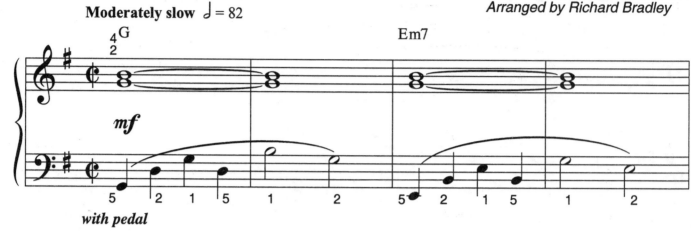

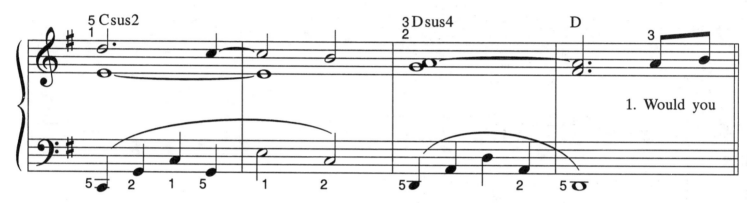

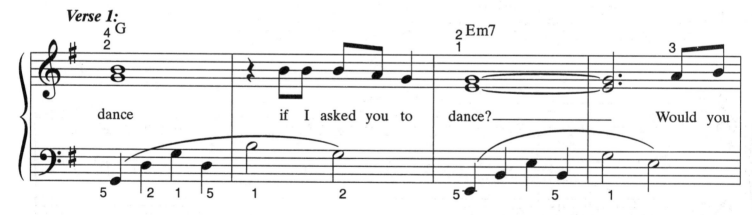

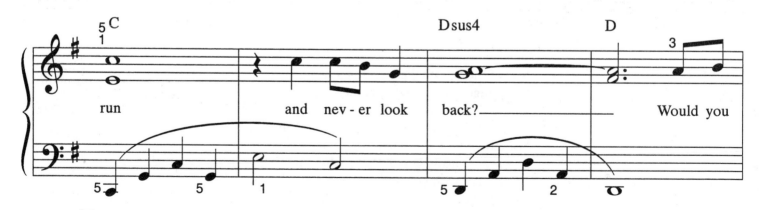

Hero - 6 - 1

88

Chorus:

Hero - 6 - 3

Verse 3:
Would you swear
That you'll always be mine?
Would you lie?
Would you run and hide?
Am I in too deep?
Have I lost my mind?
I don't care, you're here tonight.

CAN'T FIGHT THE MOONLIGHT
(THEME FROM "COYOTE UGLY")

Recorded by LeAnn Rimes

Words and Music by
DIANE WARREN
Arranged by Richard Bradley

Can't Fight the Moonlight - 6 - 1

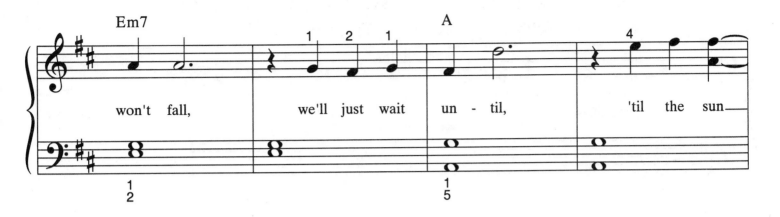

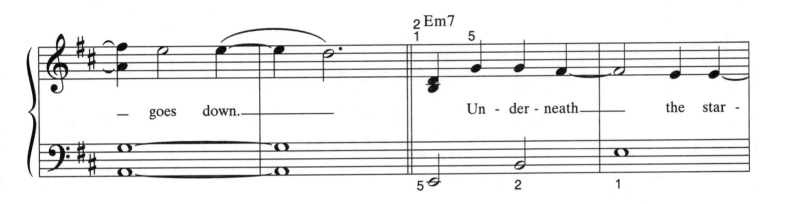

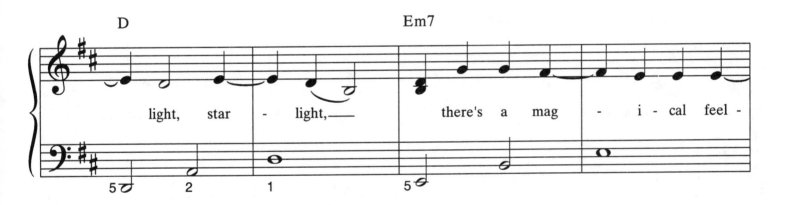

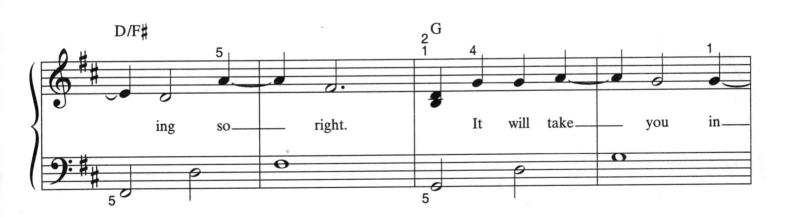

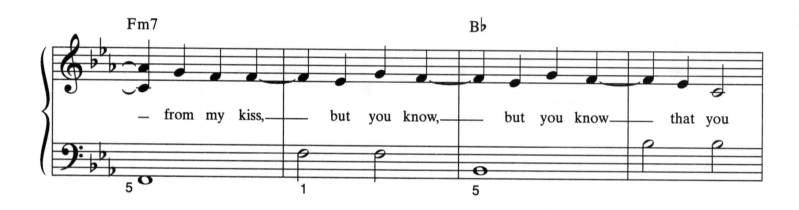

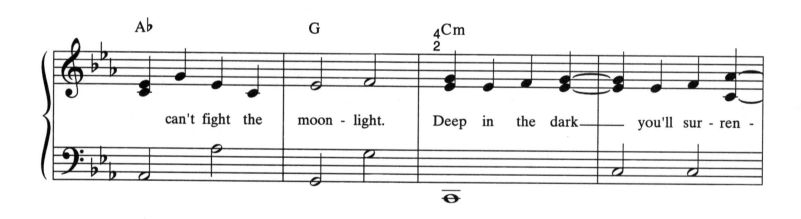

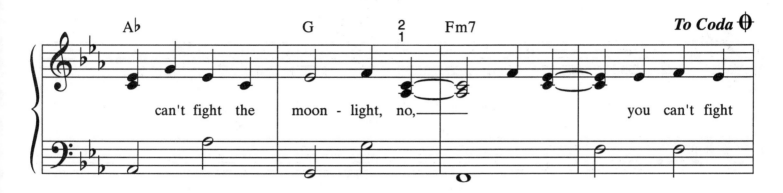

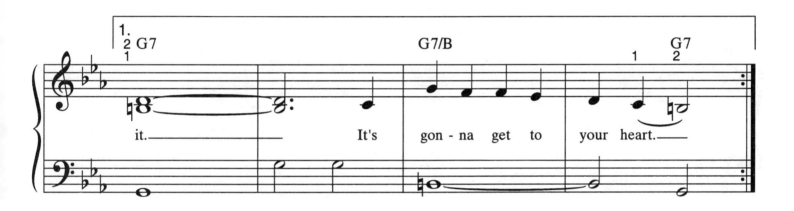

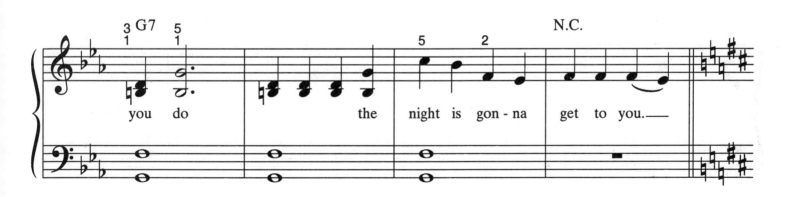

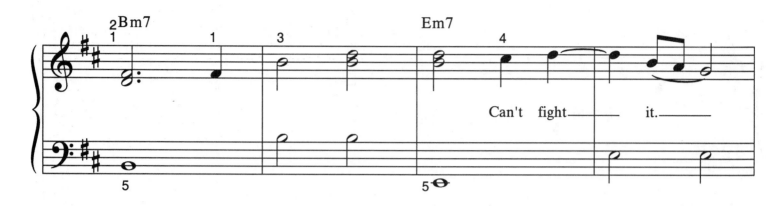

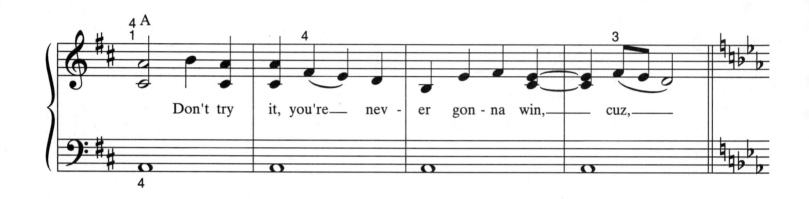

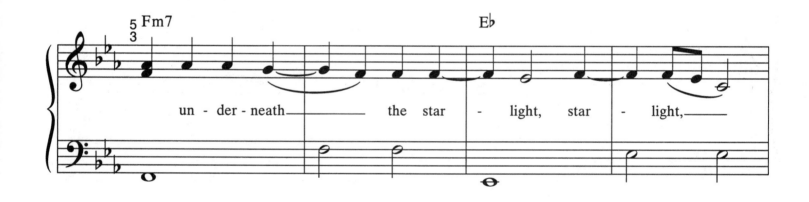

Verse 2:
There's no escape from love.
Once the gentle breeze
Weaves its spell upon your heart,
No matter what you think,
It won't be too long 'til you're in my arms.
Underneath the starlight, starlight,
We'll be lost in a rhythm so right.
Feel it steal your heart tonight.
You can try . . .
(To Chorus:)

I TURN TO YOU

Recorded by Christina Aguilera

Words and Music by
DIANE WARREN
Arranged by Richard Bradley

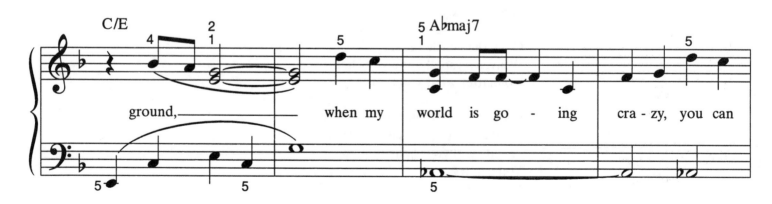

I Turn to You - 6 - 1

turn it all _____ a - round. _____   And when I'm

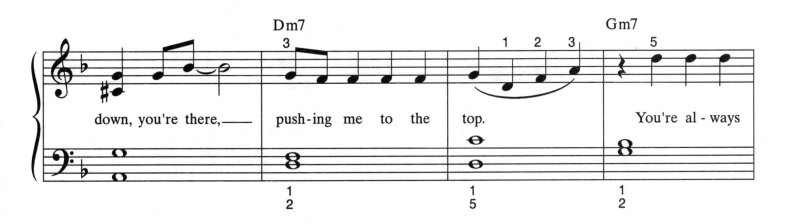

down, you're there, _____ push-ing me to the top.   You're al - ways

there giv - ing me all _____ you've ___ got. _____   For a

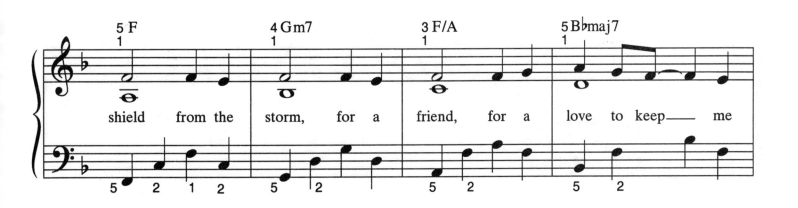

shield from the storm, for a friend, for a love to keep ___ me

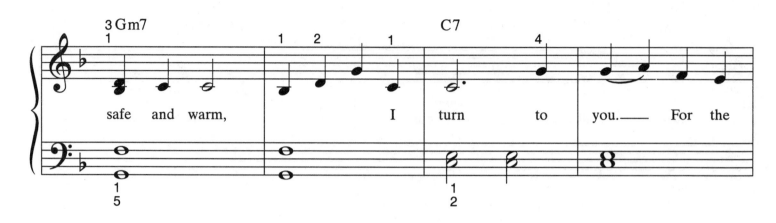

safe and warm, I turn to you.____ For the

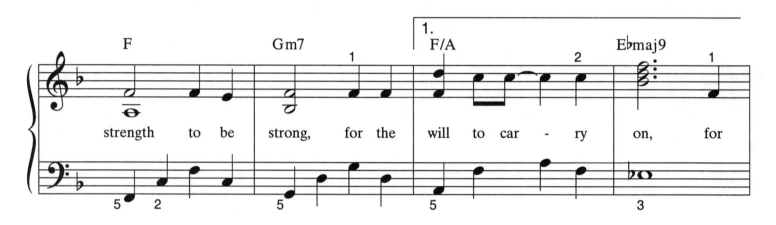

strength to be strong, for the will to car - ry on, for

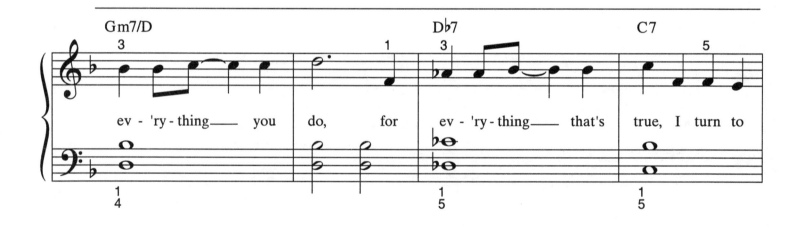

ev - 'ry-thing____ you do, for ev - 'ry-thing____ that's true, I turn to

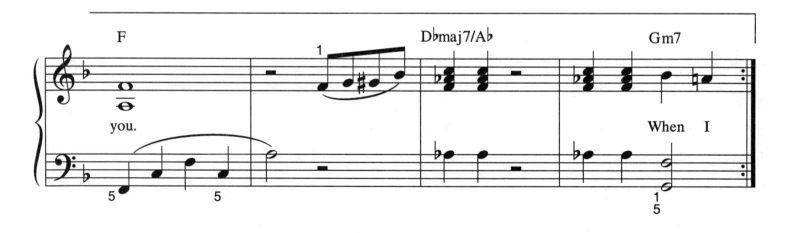

you. When I

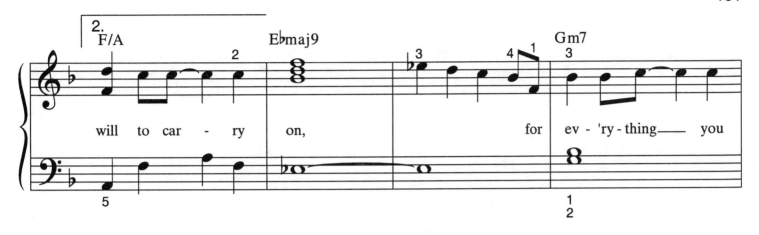

will to car - ry on, for ev - 'ry - thing____ you

do, I turn to you. For the

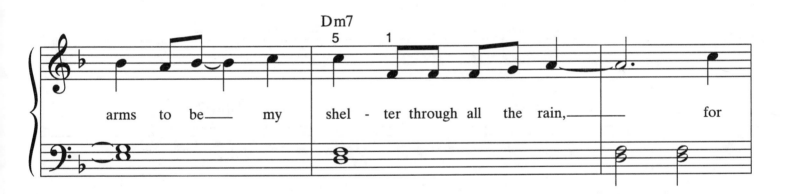

arms to be____ my shel - ter through all the rain,____ for

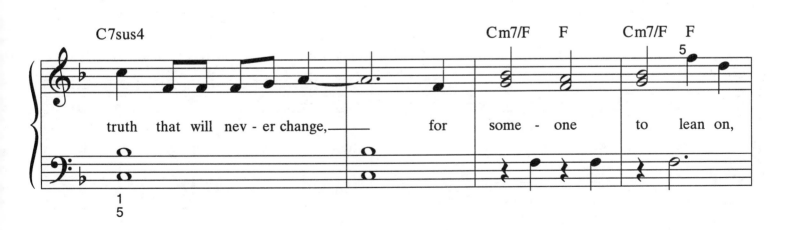

truth that will nev - er change,____ for some - one to lean on,

Verse 2:
When I lose the will to win,
I just reach for you
And I can reach the sky again.
I can do anything
'Cause your love is so amazing,
'Cause your love inspires me.
And when I need a friend,
You're always on my side,
Giving me faith,
Taking me through the night.

BACK AT ONE

Recorded by Brian McKnight

Words and Music by
BRIAN McKNIGHT
Arranged by Richard Bradley

Back at One - 4 - 2

Verse 2:
It's so incredible, the way things work themselves out.
And all emotional, once you know what it's all about, hey.
And undesirable, for us to be apart.
I never would have made it very far,
'Cause you know you've got the keys to my heart.
'Cause one, you're like a dream come true.

AND ALL THAT JAZZ

From the Academy Award winning Best Picture *Chicago*
Sung by Catherine Zeta-Jones

Words by FRED EBB
Music by JOHN KANDER
Arranged by Richard Bradley

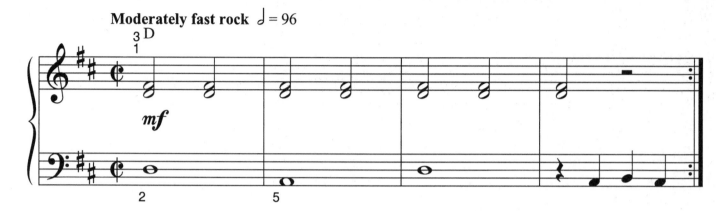

Come on, babe, — why don't we paint the town, —

and all that jazz! — I'm gon - na

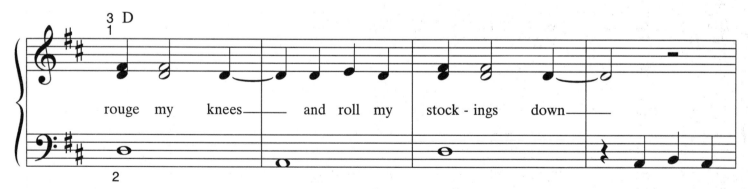

rouge my knees — and roll my stock - ings down —

And All That Jazz - 9 - 1

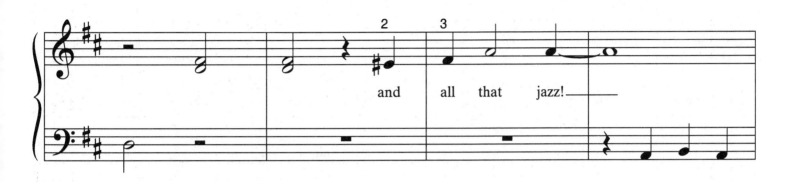

and all that jazz!

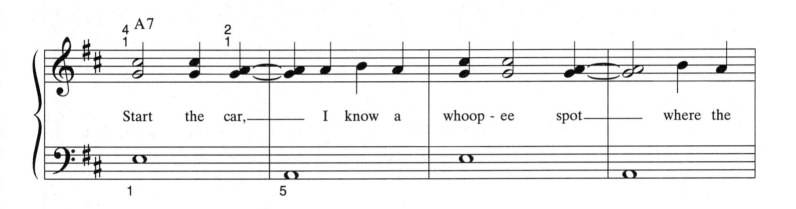

Start the car,—— I know a whoop-ee spot—— where the

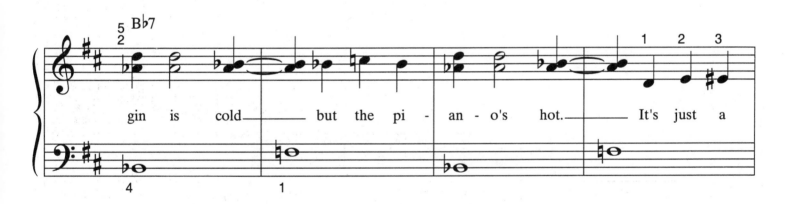

gin is cold—— but the pi-an-o's hot.—— It's just a

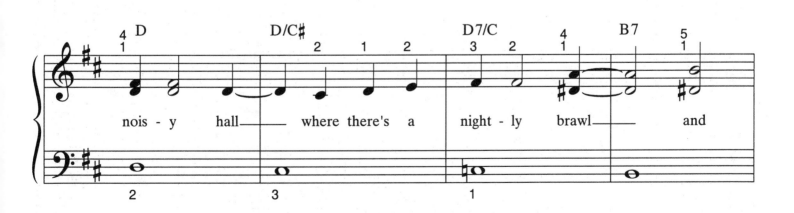

nois-y hall—— where there's a night-ly brawl—— and

oh,   I   love my life   and

all

that

jazz!

I DON'T WANT TO MISS A THING

From the Motion Picture *Armageddon*
Acedemy Award Nominee - Best Song
Recorded by Aerosmith

Words and Music by
DIANE WARREN
Arranged by Richard Bradley

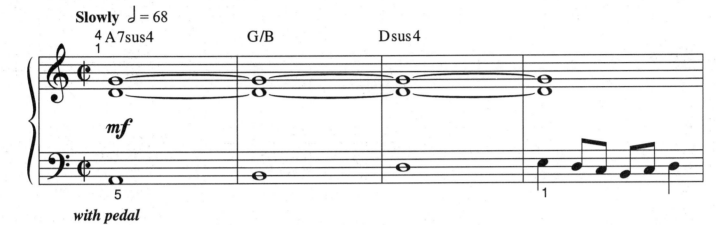

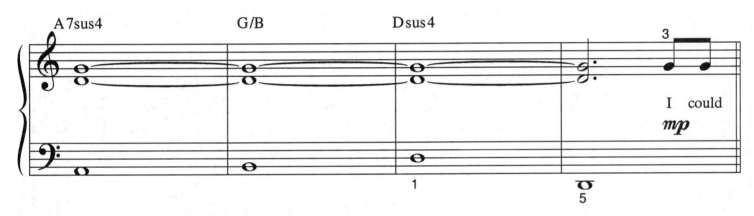

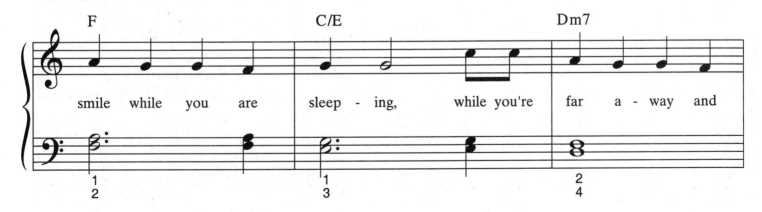

I Don't Want to Miss a Thing - 5 - 1

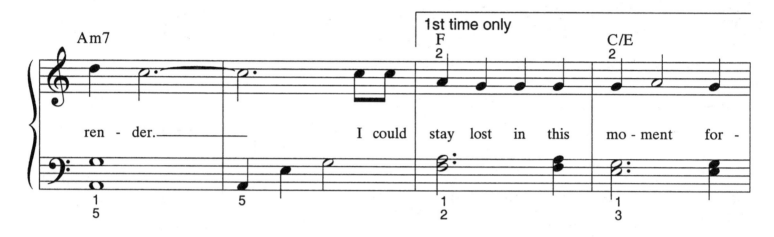

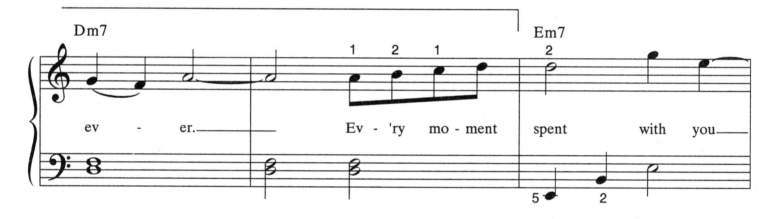

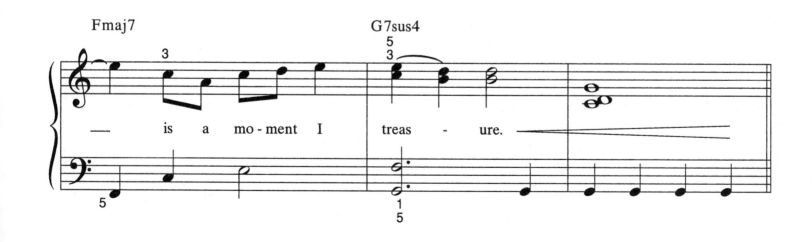

Verse 2:
Laying close to you, feeling your heart beating,
And I'm wondering what you're dreaming,
Wondering if it's me you're seeing.
Then I kiss your eyes and thank God we're together.
I just wanna stay with you in this moment together.

SOMEWHERE IN TIME
(THEME)

From the Motion Picture *Somewhere in Time*

By JOHN BARRY
Arranged by Richard Bradley

Somewhere in Time - 3 - 1

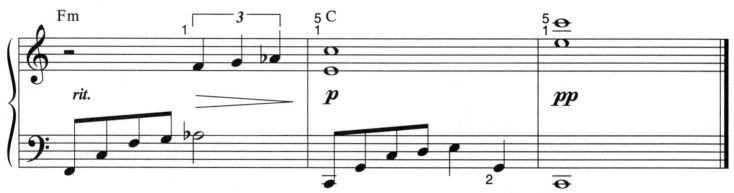

OVER THE RAINBOW

From the Motion Picture *The Wizard of Oz*
Sung by Judy Garland
Academy Award Winner - Best Song

Lyric by E.Y. HARBURG
Music by HAROLD ARLEN
Arranged by Richard Bradley

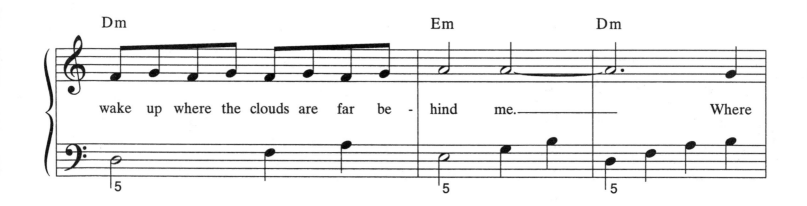

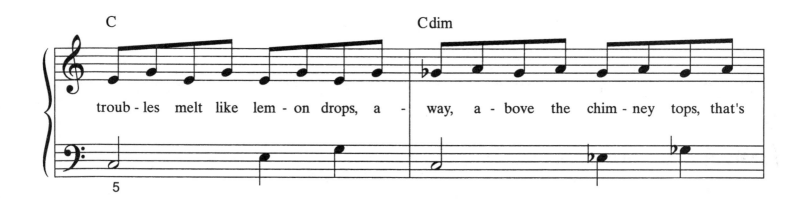

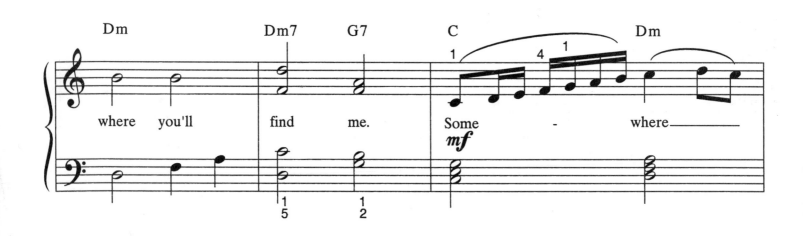

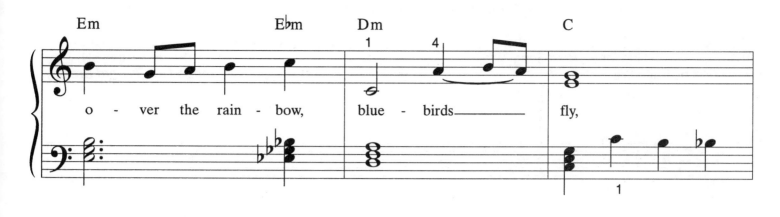

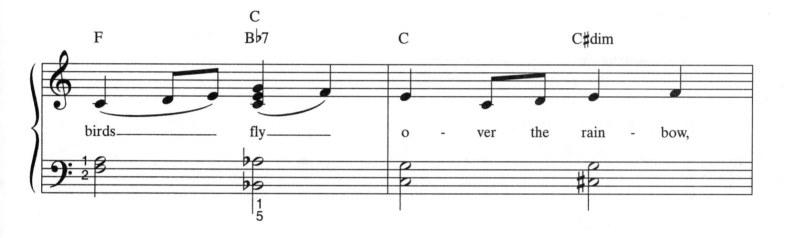

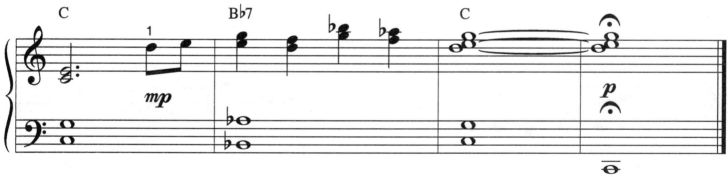

THERE YOU'LL BE

From Touchstone Pictures' *Pearl Harbor*
Academy Award Nominee - Best Song
Recorded by Faith Hill

Words and Music by
DIANE WARREN
Arranged by Richard Bradley

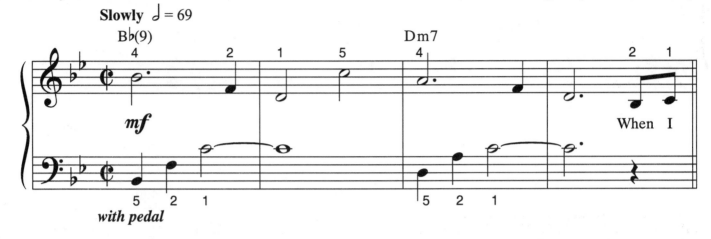

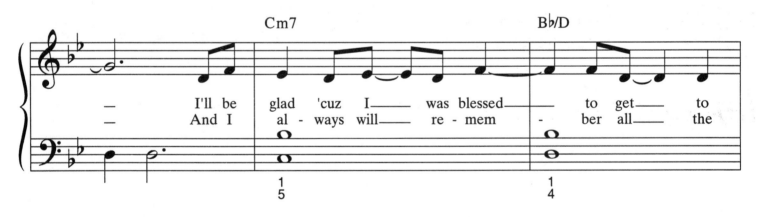

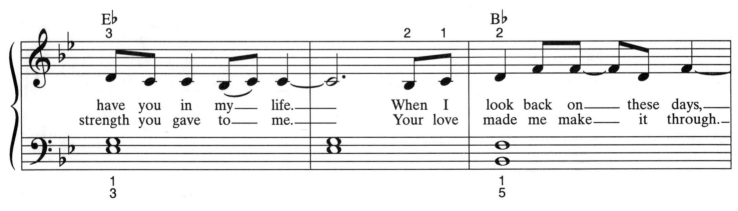

There You'll Be - 6 - 1

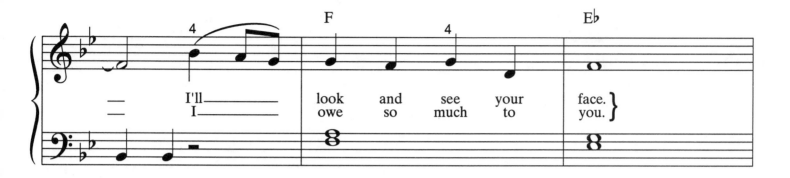

I'll_____ look and see your face.
I_____ owe so much to you.

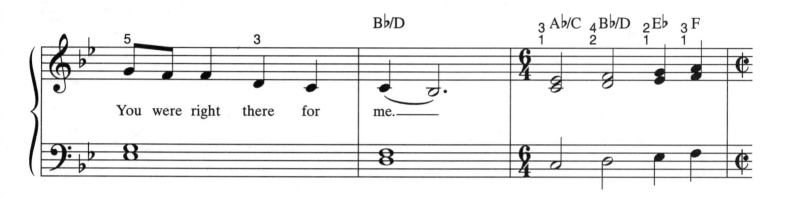

You were right there for me._____

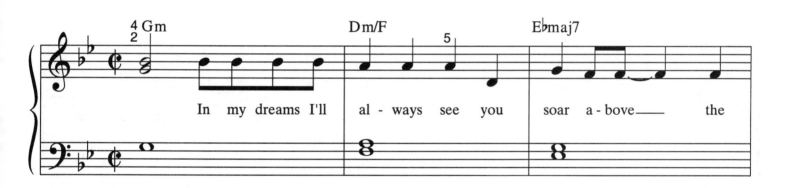

In my dreams I'll al - ways see you soar a - bove_____ the

sky._____ In my heart there'll al - ways be a

place for you____ for all my life.____ I'll keep

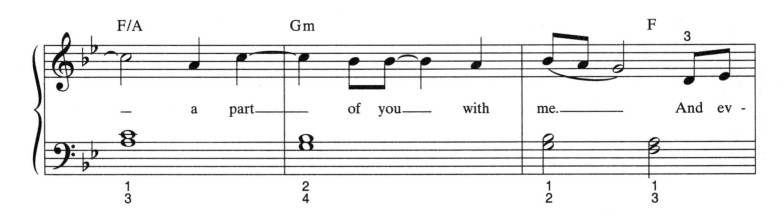

____ a part____ of you____ with me.____ And ev-

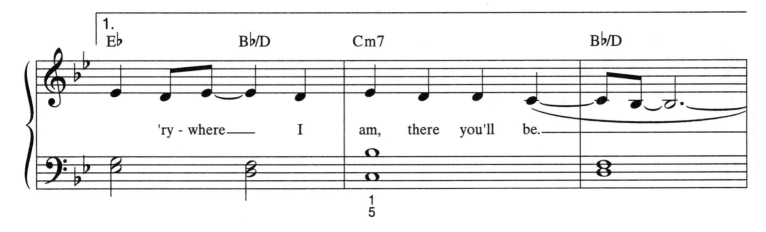

'ry-where____ I am, there you'll be.____

____ And ev-'ry-where____ I am,____ there you'll be.

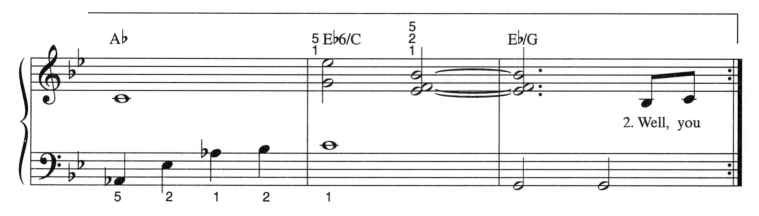

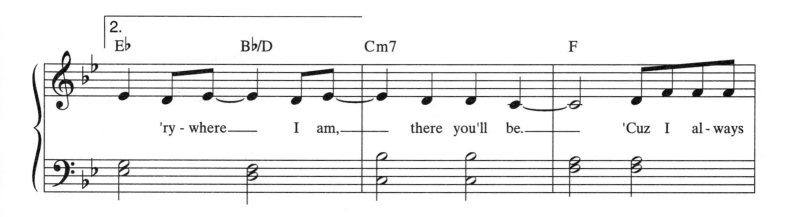

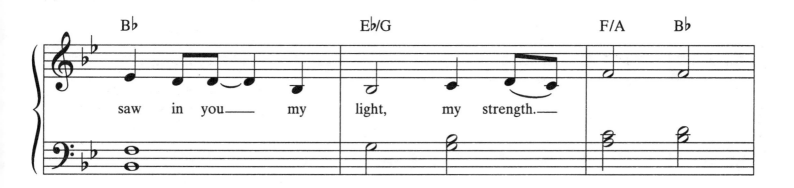

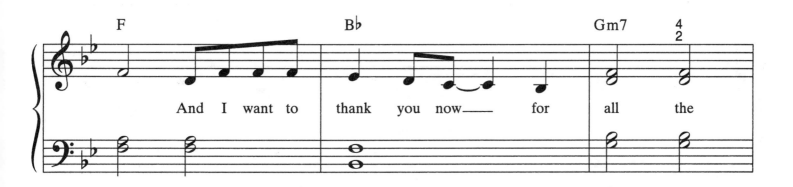

YOU LIGHT UP MY LIFE

From the Motion Picture *You Light Up My Life*
Academy Award Winner - Best Song
Sung in the Film by Didi Conn / Pop Recordings: Debby Boone, LeAnn Rimes

Words and Music by
JOE BROOKS
Arranged by Richard Bradley

You Light Up My Life - 4 - 1

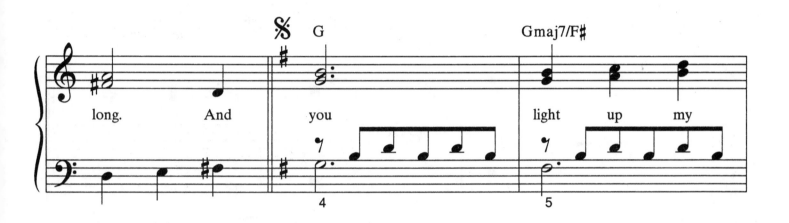

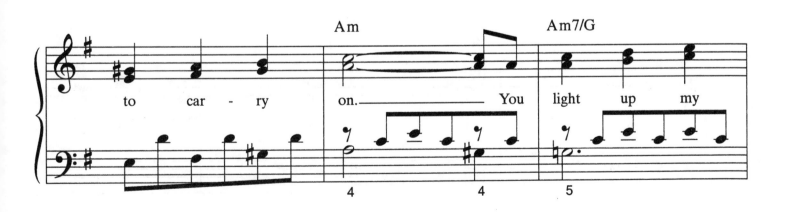

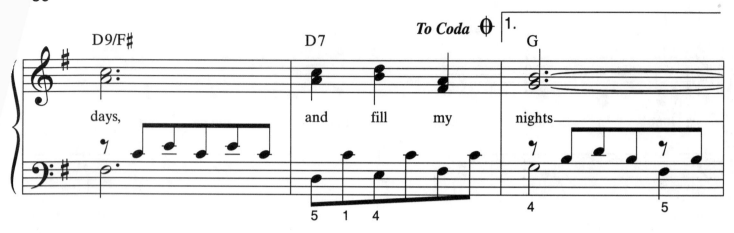

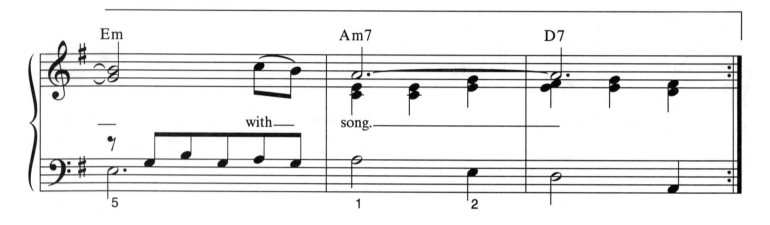

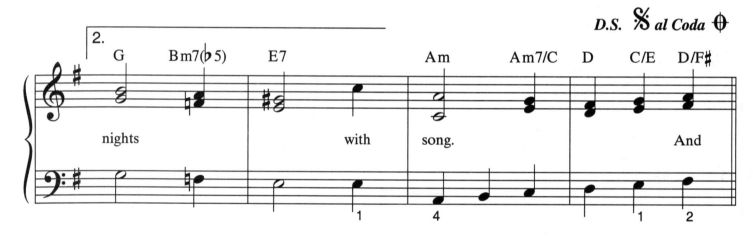

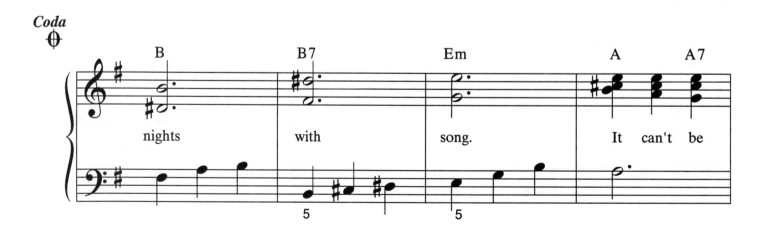

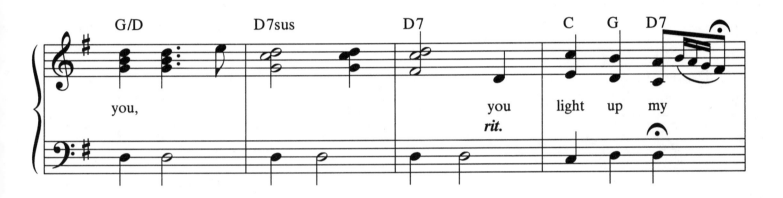

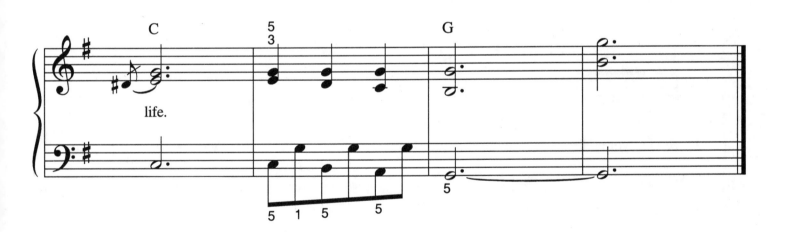

Verse 2:
Rollin' at sea, adrift on the waters,
Could it be finally I'm turning for home?
Finally a chance to say, "Hey! I love you."
Never again to be all alone.
Chorus:

ARTHUR'S THEME
(BEST THAT YOU CAN DO)

From the Motion Picture *Arthur*
Academy Award Winner - Best Song
Recorded by Christopher Cross

Words and Music by BURT BACHARACH, CAROL BAYER SAGER,
CHRISTOPHER CROSS and PETER ALLEN
Arranged by Richard Bradley

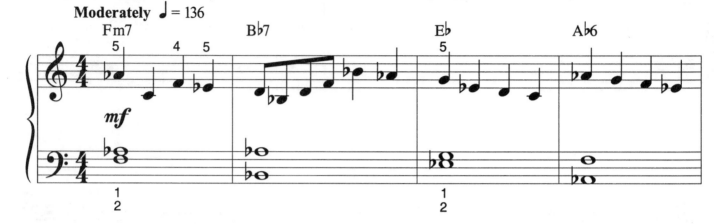

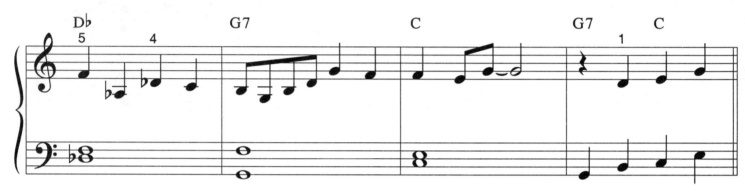

Once in your life,—— you'll find her, some - one who turns—— your

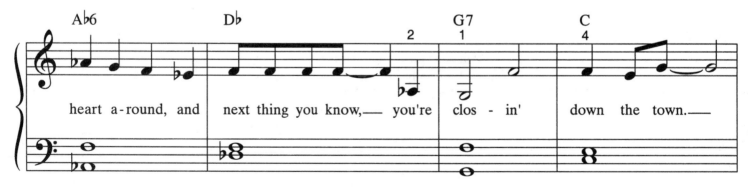

heart a - round, and next thing you know,—— you're clos - in' down the town.——

Arthur's Theme - 4 - 1

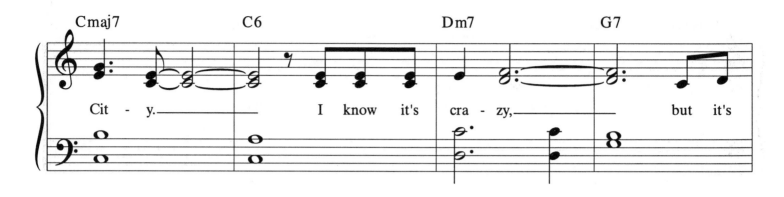

Cmaj7   C6   Dm7   G7

Cit - y.   I know it's cra - zy,   but it's

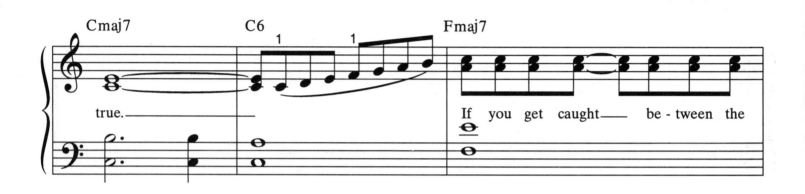

Cmaj7   C6   Fmaj7

true.   If you get caught be - tween the

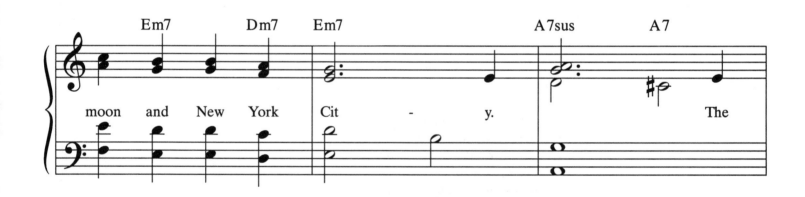

Em7   Dm7   Em7   A7sus   A7

moon and New York Cit - y.   The

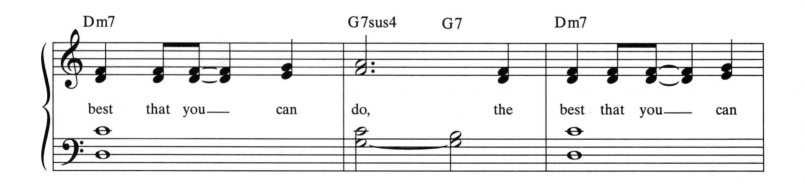

Dm7   G7sus4   G7   Dm7

best that you can do, the best that you can

do   is   fall - in'   in   love.

love.

Verse 2:
Arthur he does what he pleases.
All of his life his master's toys,
And deep in his heart, he's just,
He's just a boy.
Livin' his life one day at a time
He's showing himself a really good time.
He's laughin' about the way they want him to be.

RAINDROPS KEEP FALLIN' ON MY HEAD

From the Motion Picture *Butch Cassidy and the Sundance Kid*
Academy Award Winner - Best Song
Recorded by B. J. Thomas

Words by HAL DAVID
Music by BURT BACHARACH
Arranged by Richard Bradley

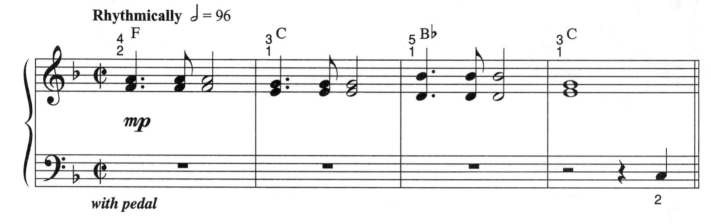

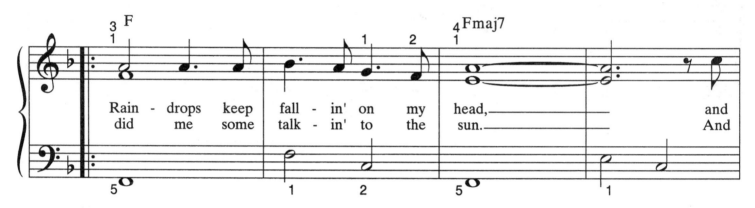

Rain - drops keep fall - in' on my head,_____ and
did me some talk - in' to the sun._____ And

just like the guy whose feet are too big for his
I said I did - n't like the way he got his things

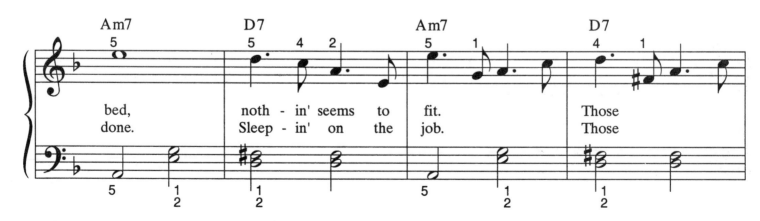

bed, noth - in' seems to fit. Those
done. Sleep - in' on the job. Those

Raindrops Keep Fallin' on My Head - 4 - 1

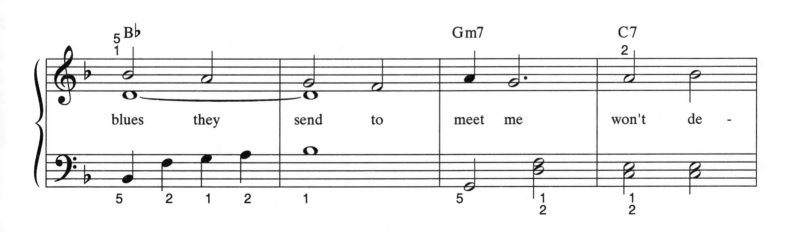

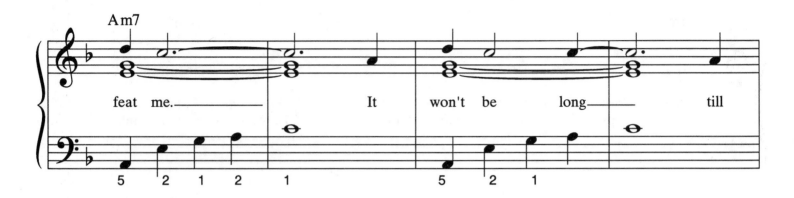

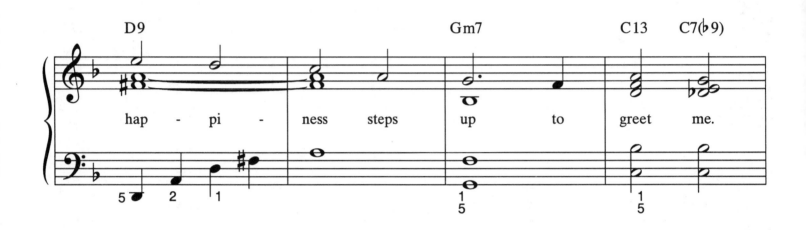

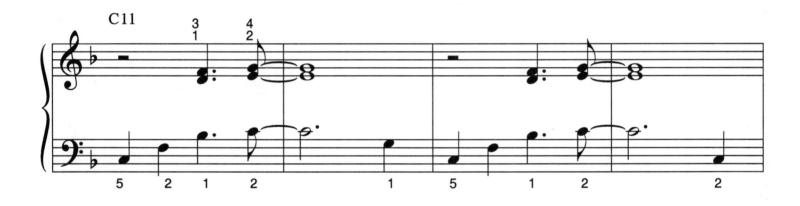

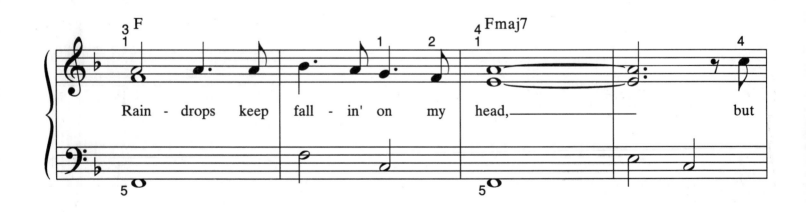

SOMEWHERE OUT THERE

From the Motion Picture *An American Tail*
Academy Award Nominee - Best Song
Recorded by Linda Ronstadt and James Ingram

By JAMES HORNER, BARRY MANN
and CYNTHIA WEIL
Arranged by Richard Bradley

Moderately, with expression ♩ = 96

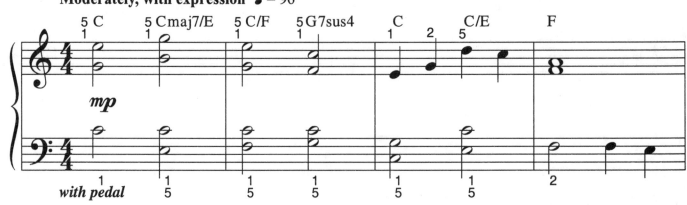

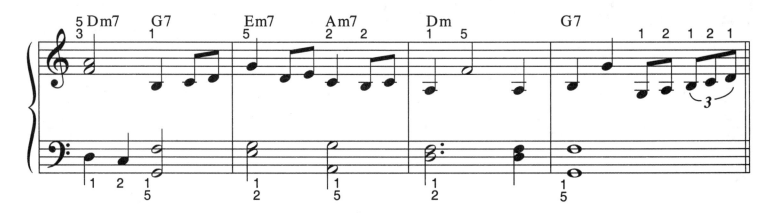

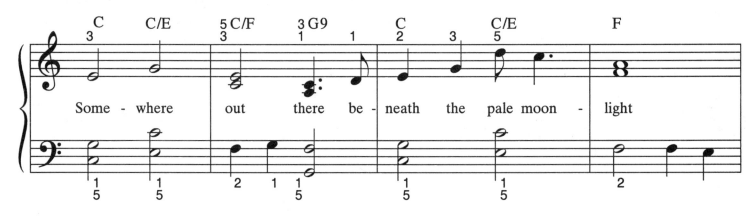

Some - where   out   there   be - neath   the   pale   moon - light

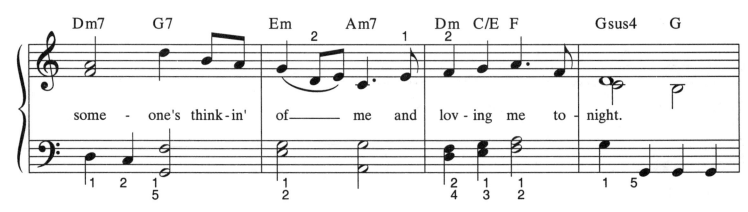

some - one's think-in'   of____   me   and   lov - ing   me   to - night.

Somewhere Out There - 4 - 1

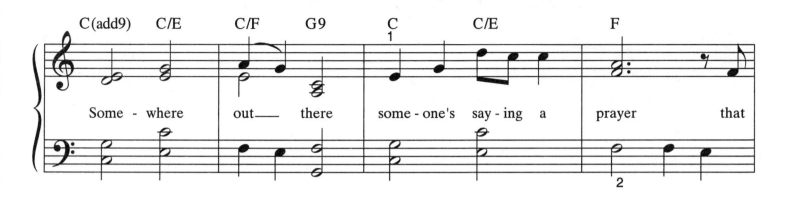

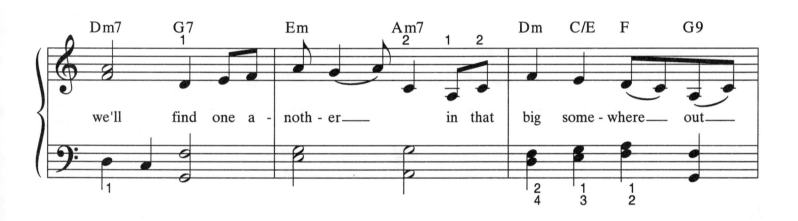

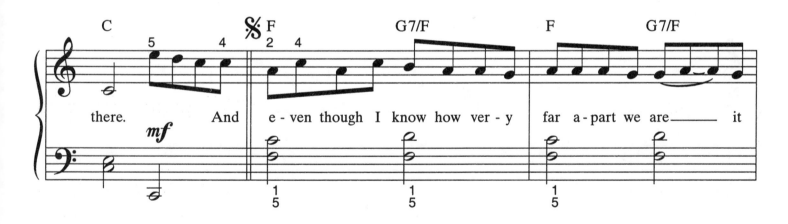

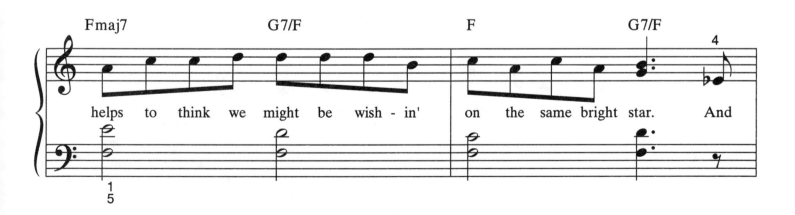

when the night wind starts to sing a lone-some lul-la-by it

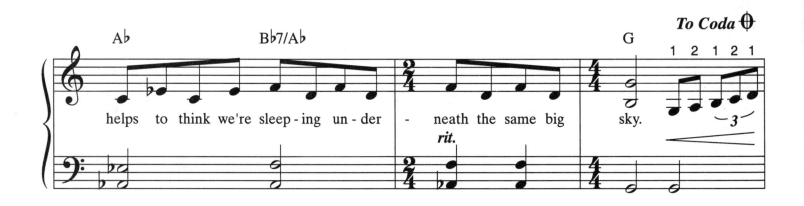

helps to think we're sleep-ing un-der - neath the same big sky.

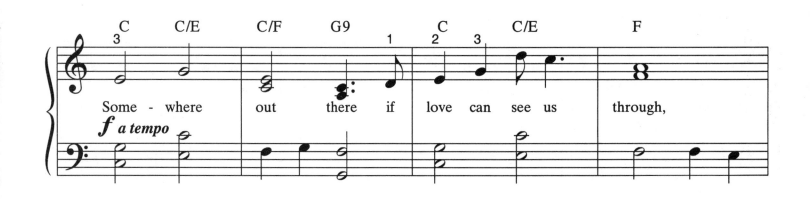

Some - where out there if love can see us through,

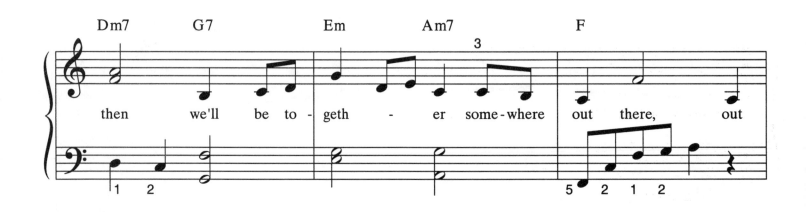

then we'll be to - geth - er some-where out there, out

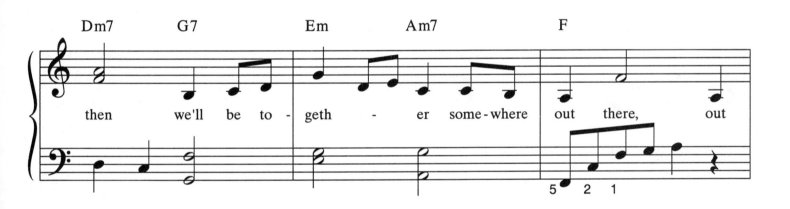

BECAUSE YOU LOVED ME

Theme from *Up Close & Personal*
Academy Award Nominee - Best Song
Recorded by Celine Dion

Words and Music by
DIANE WARREN
Arranged by Richard Bradley

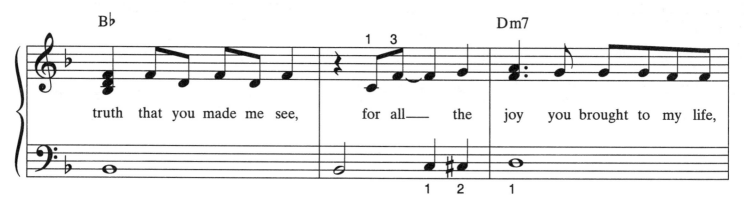

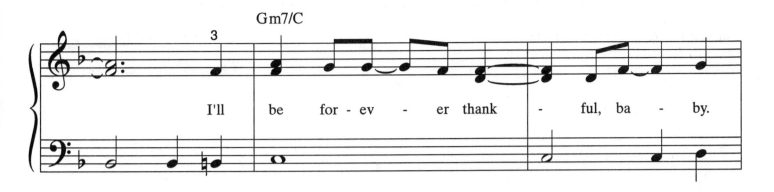

I'll be for - ev - er thank - ful, ba - by.

You're the one who held me up, nev-er let me fall.

You're the one who saw me through, through it all.

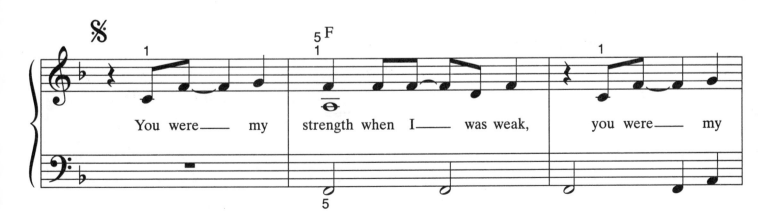

You were my strength when I was weak, you were my

Verse 2:
You gave me wings and made me fly,
You touched my hand, I could touch the sky.
I lost my faith, you gave it back to me.
You said no star was out of reach,
You stood by me and I stood tall.
I had your love, I had it all.
I'm grateful for each day you gave me.
Maybe I don't know that much,
But I know this much is true.
I was blessed because I was loved by you.

STAR WARS
(MAIN THEME)

From the Motion Picture *Star Wars*
Acedemy Award Winner - Best Score

Music by
JOHN WILLIAMS
Arranged by Richard Bradley

Majestic ♩ = 92
C/D
D
C/D
f
with pedal
D
G
C
G
C
G
F
D
G
C
G
C
G
F
D
mp

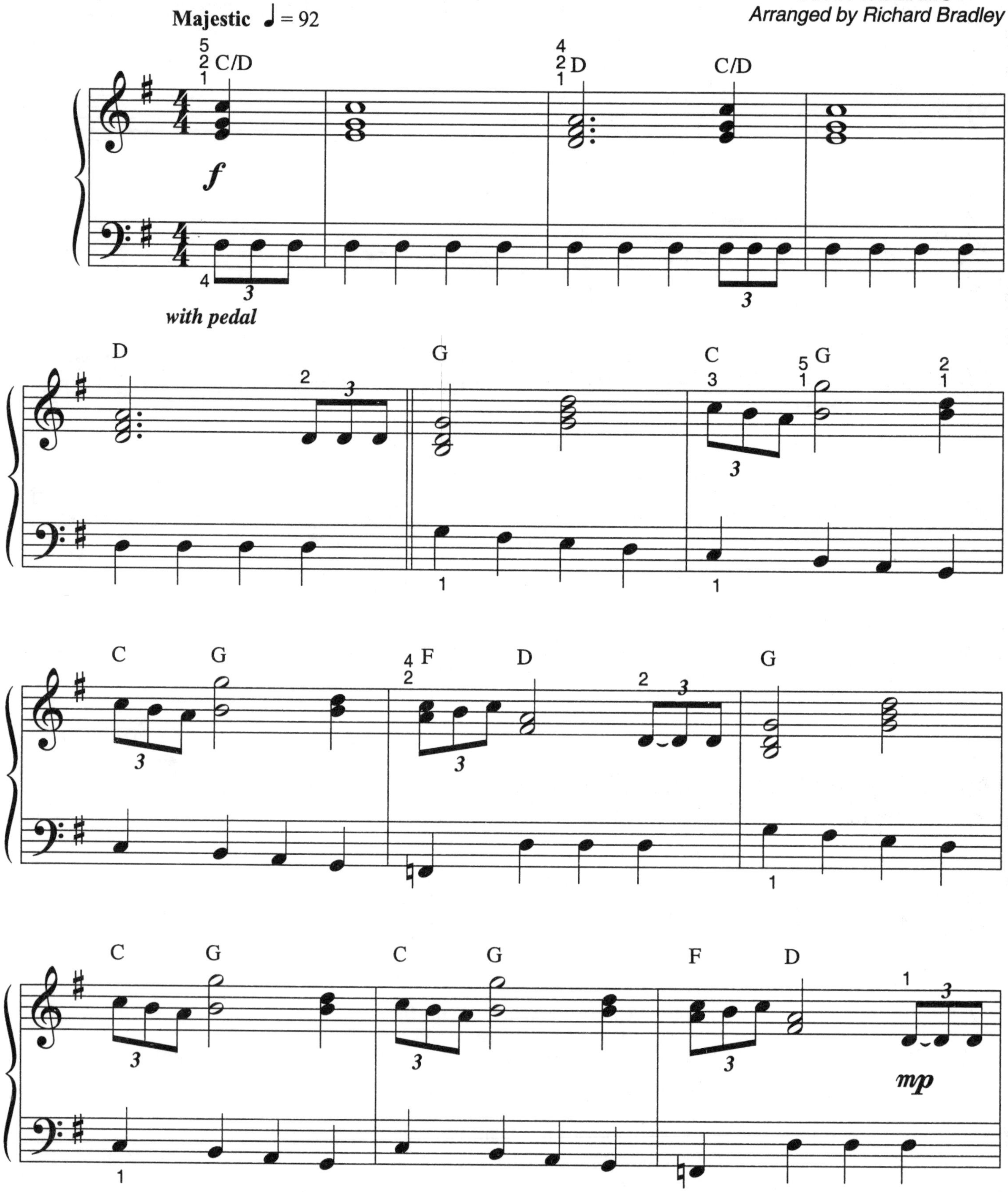

THE ROSE

From the Motion Picture *The Rose*
Recorded by Bette Midler

Words and Music by
AMANDA McBROOM
Arranged by Richard Bradley

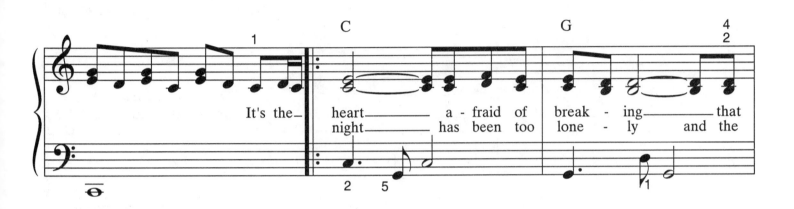

UP WHERE WE BELONG

From the Motion Picture *An Officer and a Gentleman*
Academy Award Winner - Best Song
Recorded by Joe Cocker & Jennifer Warnes

Words by WILL JENNINGS
Music by JACK NITZSCHE and BUFFY SAINTE-MARIE
Arranged by Richard Bradley

Up Where We Belong - 5 - 1

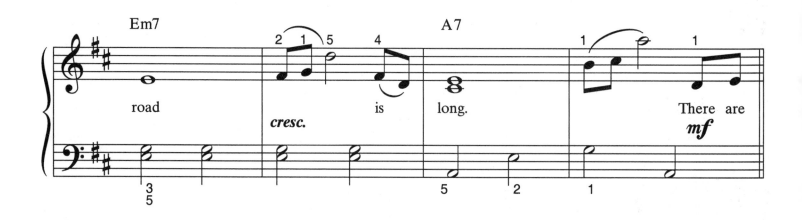

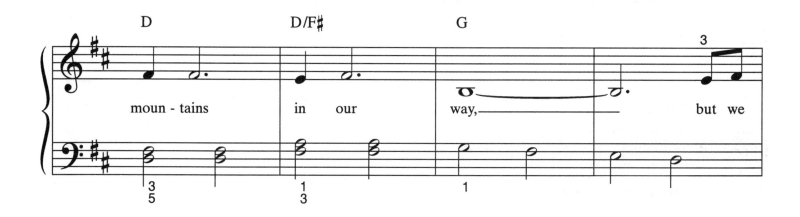

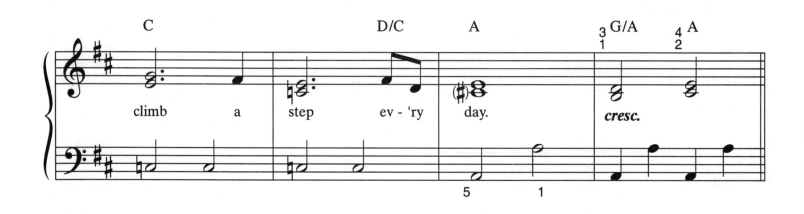

Verse 2:
Some hang on to "used-to-be",
Live their lives looking behind.
All we have is here and now;
All our life, out there to find.
The road is long.
There are mountains in our way,
But we climb them a step every day.

AS TIME GOES BY

From the Motion Picture *Casablanca*.
Performed in the film by Dooley Wilson

Words and Music by
HERMAN HUPFELD
Arranged by Richard Bradley

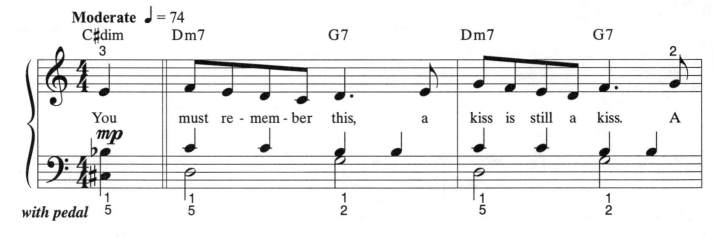

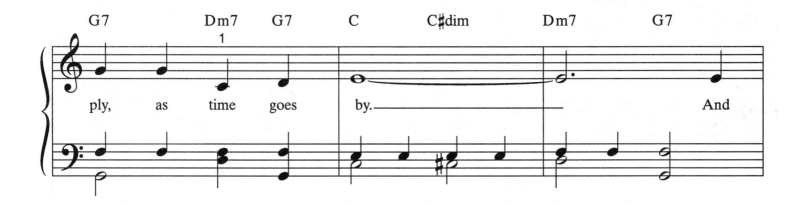

As Time Goes By - 4 - 1

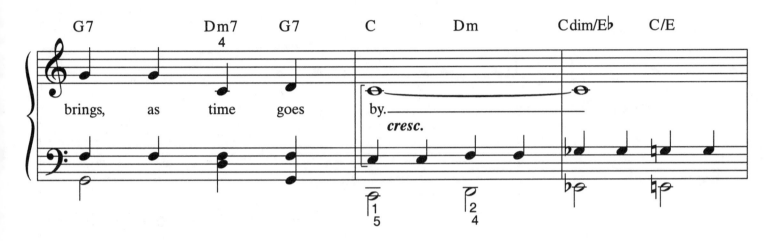

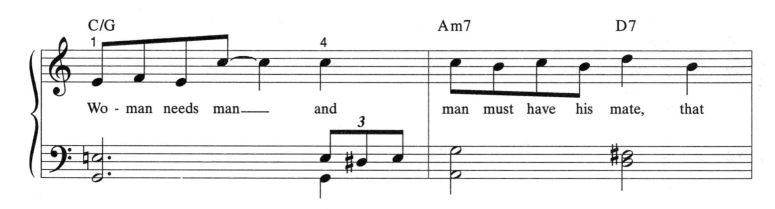

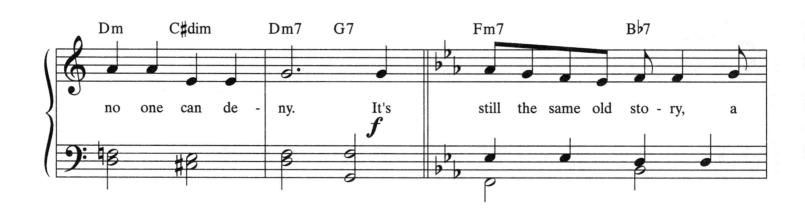

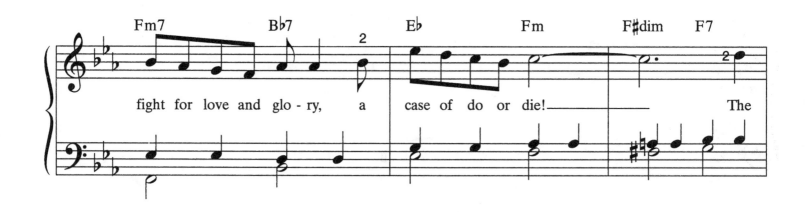

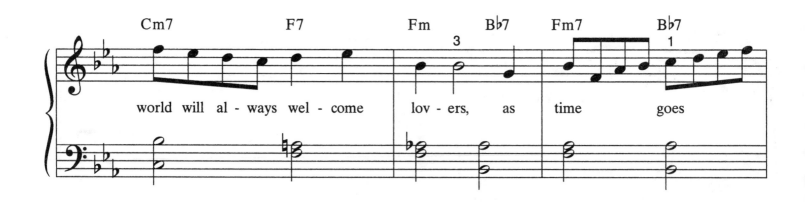

MUSIC OF MY HEART

From the Miramax Picture *Music of the Heart*
Academy Award Nominee - Best Song
Recorded by Gloria Estefan and ★NSYNC

Words and Music by
DIANE WARREN
Arranged by Richard Bradley

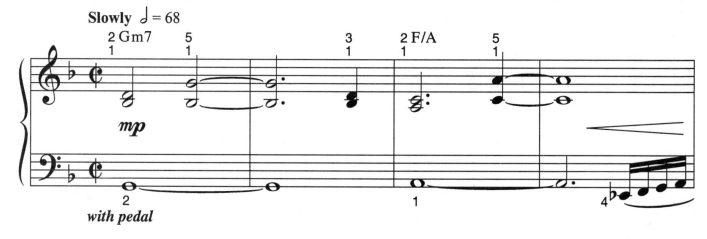

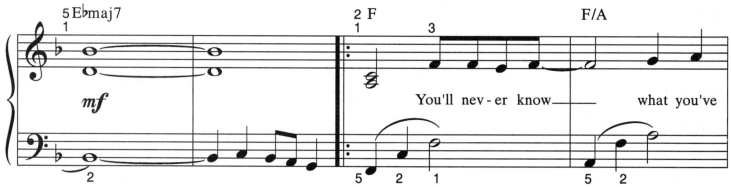

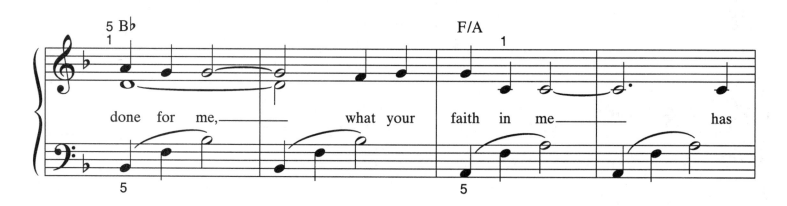

Music of My Heart - 6 - 1

giv - en me. I'll car - ry it with me.

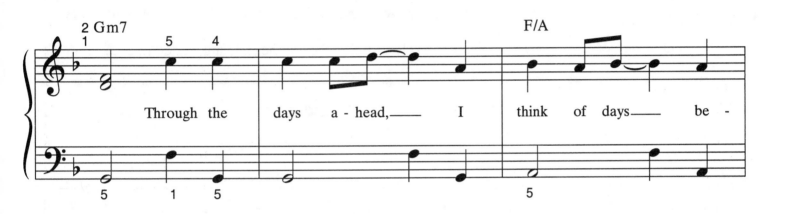

Through the days a - head, I think of days be -

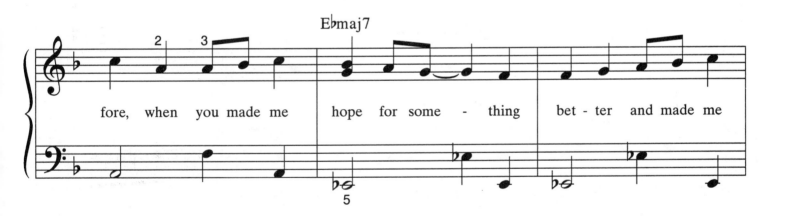

fore, when you made me hope for some - thing bet - ter and made me

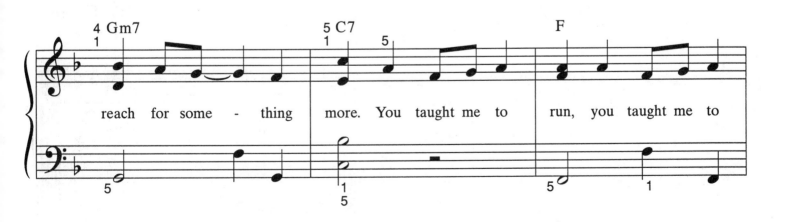

reach for some - thing more. You taught me to run, you taught me to

Verse 2:
You were the one always on my side,
Always standing by, seeing me through.
You were the song that always made me sing.
I'm singing this for you.
Everywhere I go, I think of where I've been
And of the one who knew me better
Than anyone ever will again.

HOW DO I LIVE

From the Motion Picture *Con Air*
Academy Award Nominee - Best Song
Soundtrack Recording by Trisha Yearwood
Popular Recording by LeAnn Rimes

Words and Music by
DIANE WARREN
Arranged by Richard Bradley

Moderately slow ♩ = 84

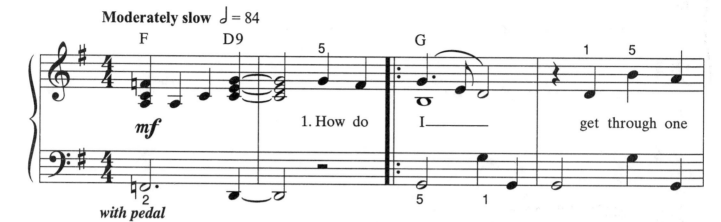

with pedal

1. How do I___ get through one

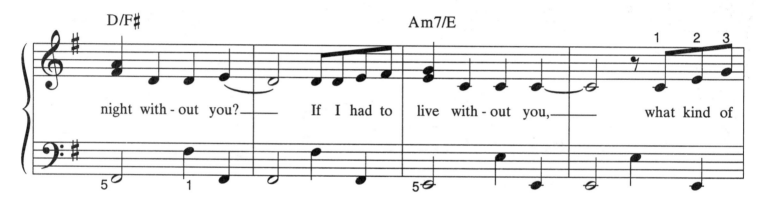

night with - out you?___ If I had to live with - out you,___ what kind of

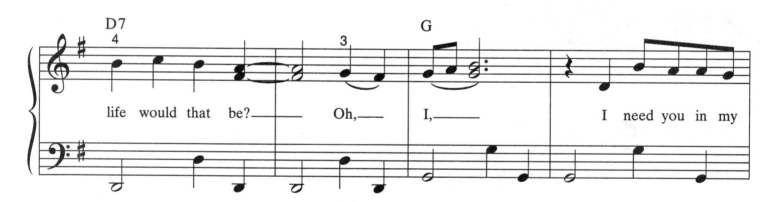

life would that be?___ Oh,___ I,___ I need you in my

arms, need you___ to hold. You're my world, my heart,___ my

How Do I Live - 5 - 1

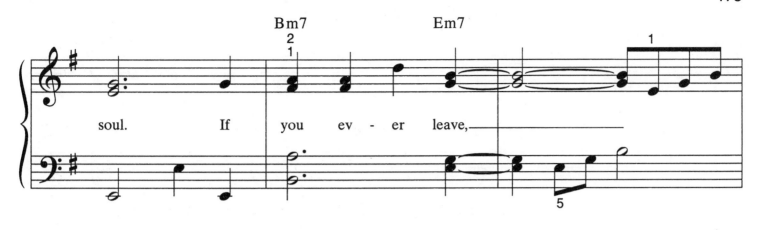

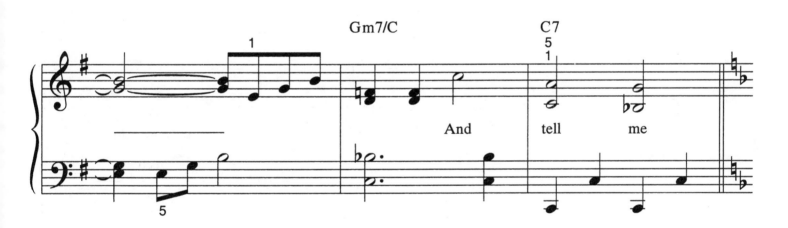

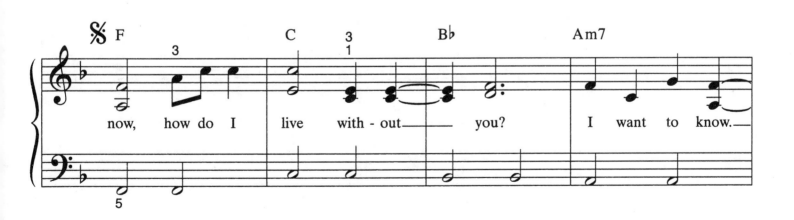

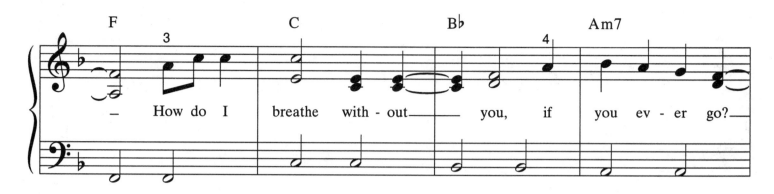

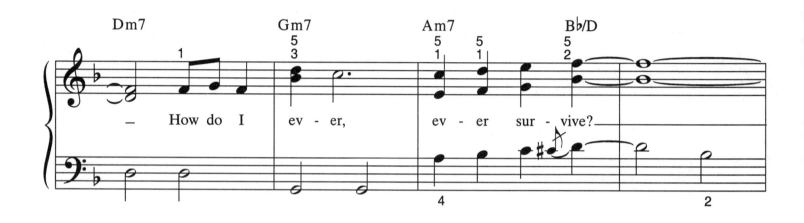

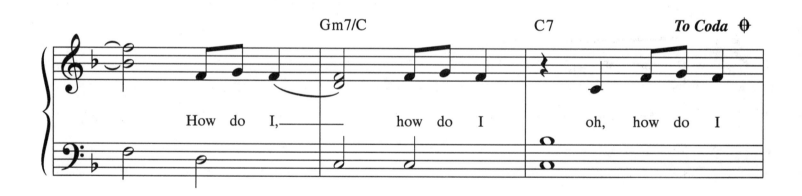

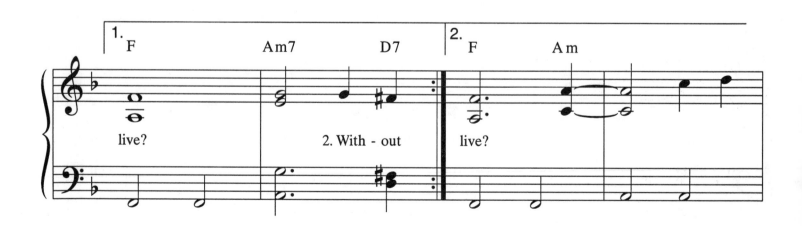

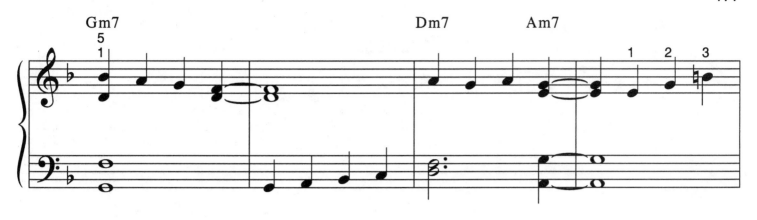

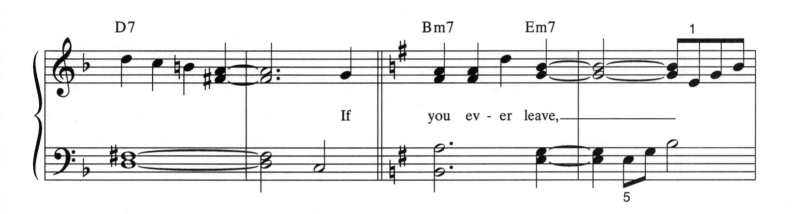

If you ev - er leave,

ba - by, you would take a - way ev - 'ry - thing. Need you with me,

ba - by, 'cause you know that you're ev - 'ry - thing

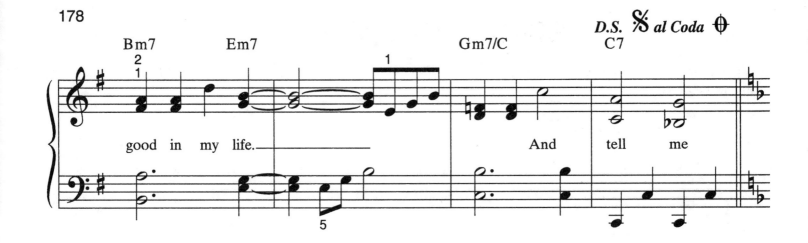

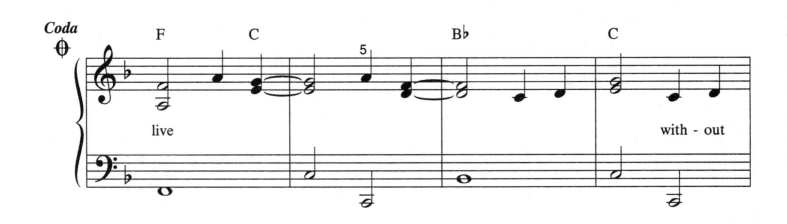

Verse 2:
Without you, there'd be no sun in my sky,
There would be no love in my life,
There'd be no world left for me.
And I, baby, I don't know what I would do,
I'd be lost if I lost you.
If you ever leave,
Baby, you would take away everything real in my life,
And tell me now. . .
(To Chorus:).

SINGIN' IN THE RAIN

From the Motion Picture *Singin' in the Rain*
Sung by Gene Kelly

Lyric by ARTHUR FREED
Music by NACIO HERB BROWN
Arranged by Richard Bradley

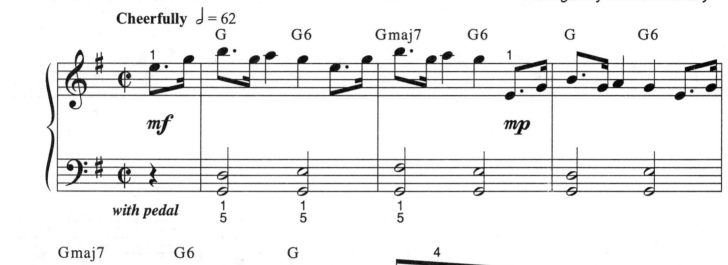

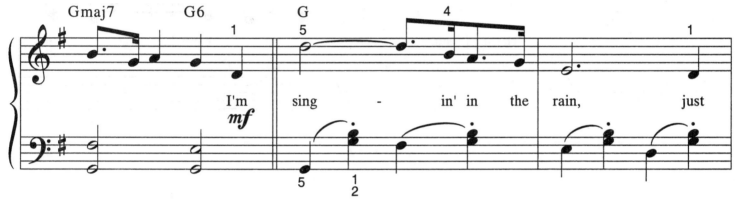

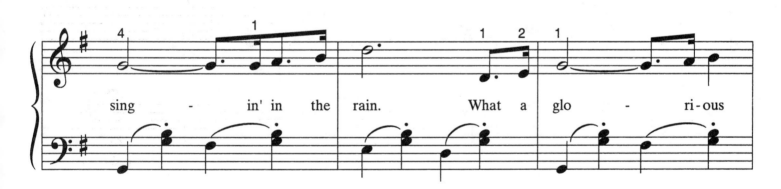

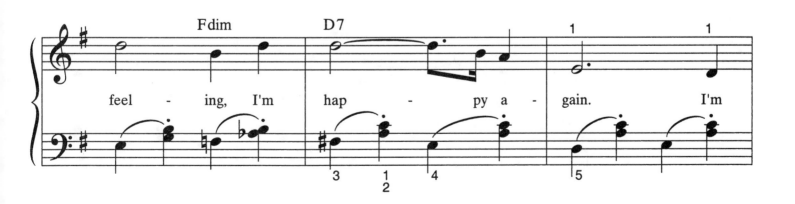

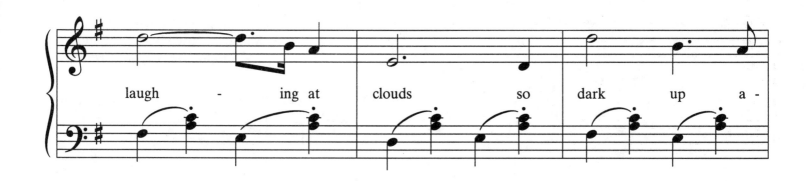

laugh - ing at clouds so dark up a -

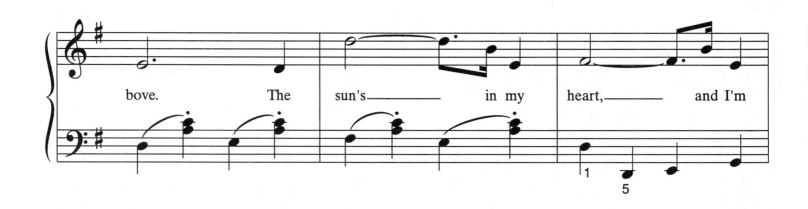

bove. The sun's in my heart, and I'm

read - y for love. Let the storm - y clouds

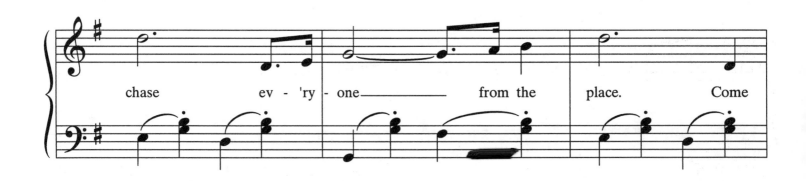

chase ev - 'ry - one from the place. Come

Singin' in the Rain - 3 - 2

THE PINK PANTHER

From the Motion Picture *The Pink Panther*
Academy Award Nominee - Best Score

Music by
HENRY MANCINI
Arranged by Richard Bradley

HOW DO YOU KEEP THE MUSIC PLAYING?

From the Motion Picture *Best Friends*
Academy Award Nominee - Best Song
Recorded by Patti Austin and James Ingram

Words by ALAN and MARILYN BERGMAN
Music by MICHEL LEGRAND
Arranged by Richard Bradley

Moderately slow ♩ = 106

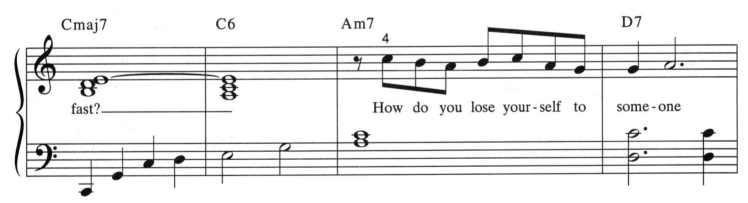

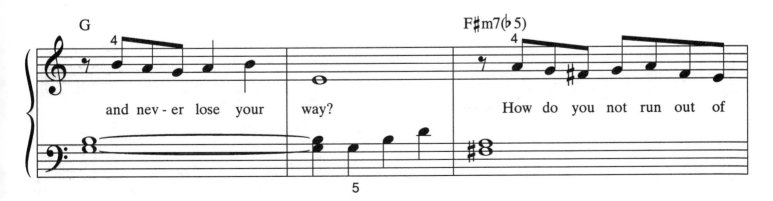

How Do You Keep the Music Playing? - 3 - 1

THEME FROM ICE CASTLES
(THROUGH THE EYES OF LOVE)

From the Mition Picture *Ice Castles*
Academy Award Nominee - Best Song
Recorded by Melissa Manchester

Lyrics by CAROL BAYER SAGER
Music by MARVIN HAMLISCH
Arranged by Richard Bradley

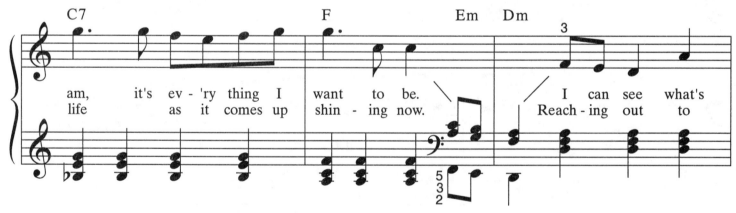

Theme from Ice Castles - 4 - 1

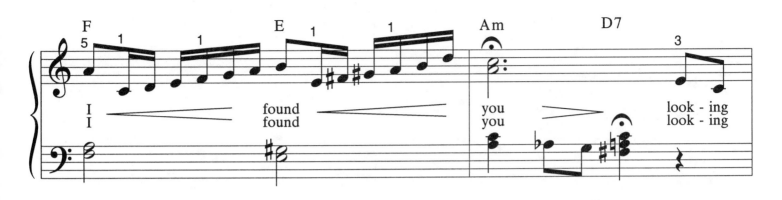

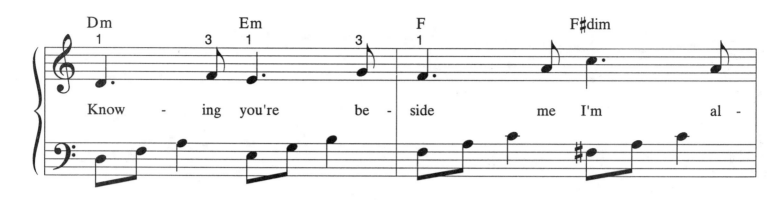

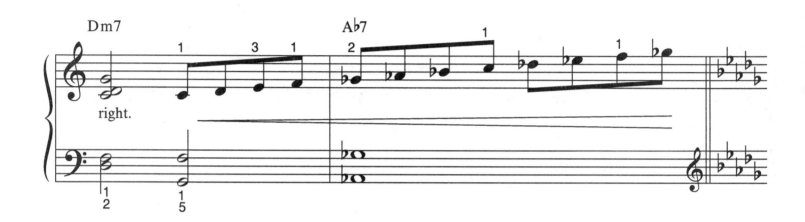

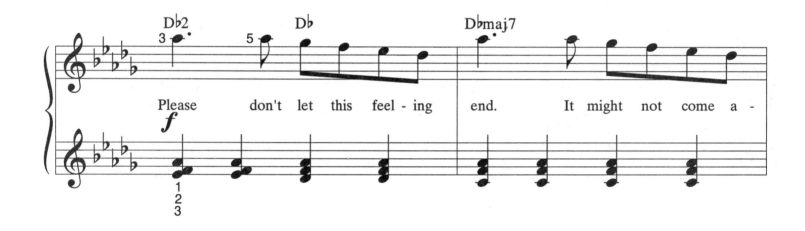

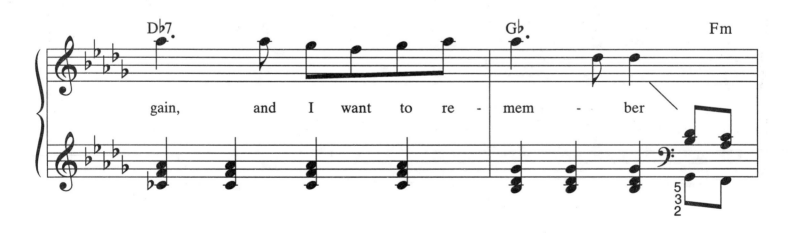

Theme from Ice Castles - 4 - 4

CANON IN D

Used as the theme for the Motion Picture *Ordinary People*

German organist - composer
1653 – 1706

JOHANN PACHELBEL
Arranged by Richard Bradley

Canon in D - 4 - 1

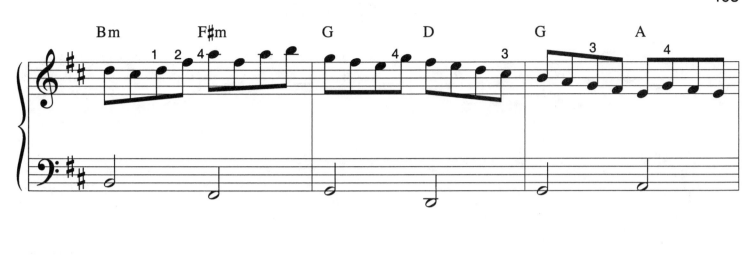

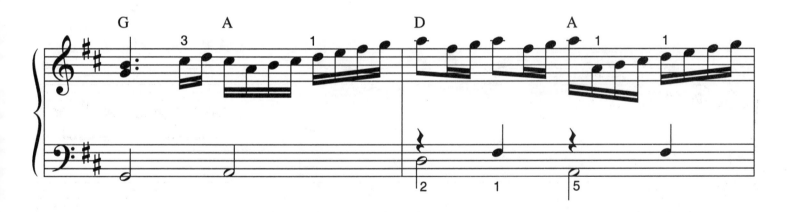

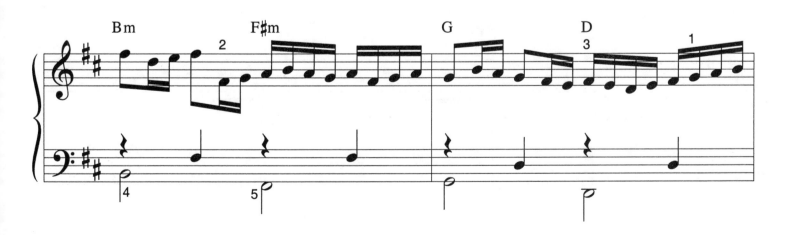

Canon in D - 4 - 3

Canon in D - 4 - 4

THE FLIGHT OF THE BUMBLE-BEE

Russian composer
1844 – 1908

N. RIMSKY-KORSAKOV
Arranged by Richard Bradley

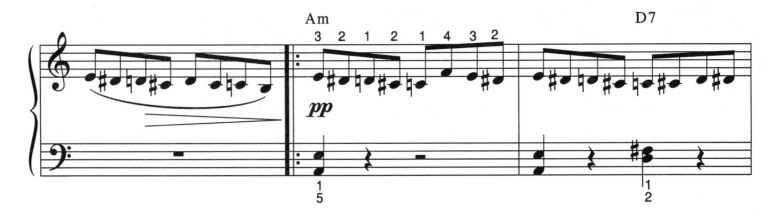

The Flight of the Bumble-Bee - 4 - 1

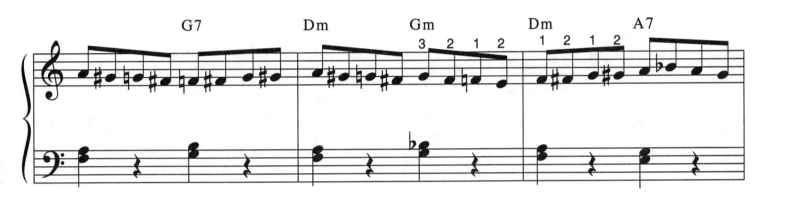

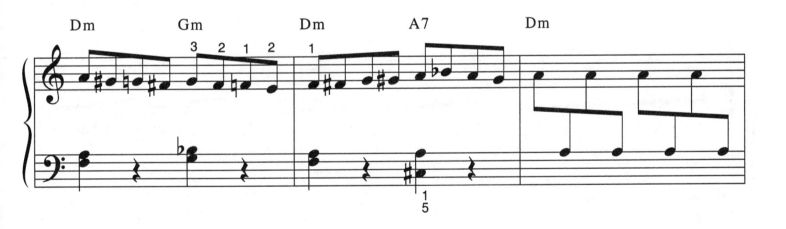

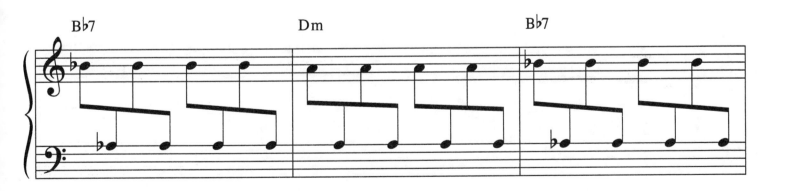

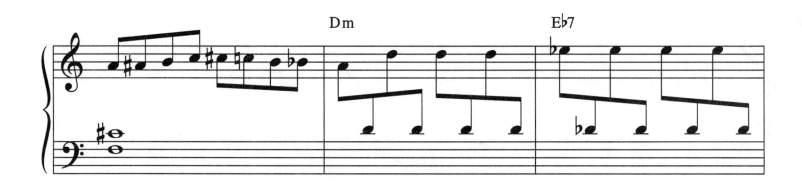

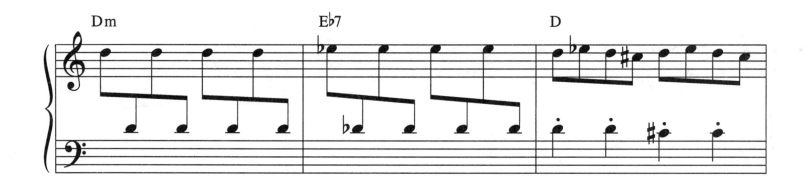

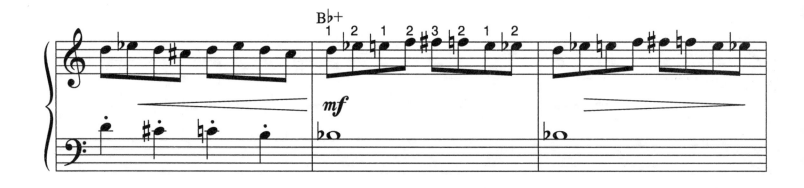

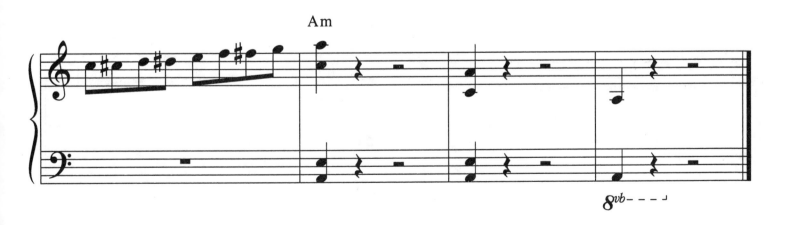

The Flight of the Bumble-Bee - 4 - 4

THE SORCERER'S APPRENTICE

Used in the Motion Picture *Walt Disney's Fantasia*

French composer
1865 – 1935

PAUL DUKAS
Arranged by Richard Bradley

The Sorcerer's Apprentice - 3 - 1

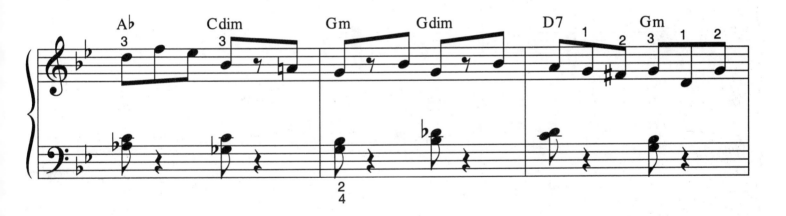

COMEDIAN'S GALLOP

Russian composer
1904 – 1987

DMITRI KABALEVSKY
Arranged by Richard Bradley

Comedians' Gallop - 3 - 1

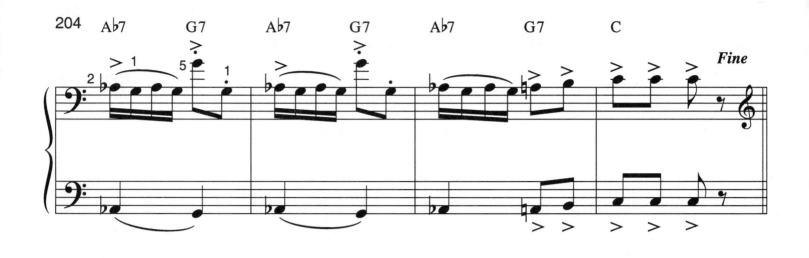

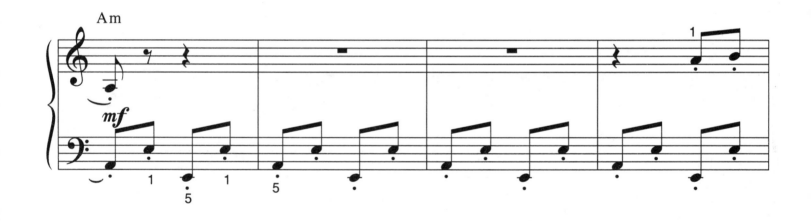

Comedians' Gallop - 3 - 2

FÜR ELISE
(MAIN THEME)

German composer
1770 – 1827

LUDWIG van BEETHOVEN
Edited by Richard Bradley

Für Elise - 2 - 1

MOONLIGHT SONATA
(Op. 27, No. 2)

German composer
1770 – 1827

LUDWIG van BEETHOVEN
Arranged by Richard Bradley

Moonlight Sonata - 4 - 1

UN BEL DI

From the opera *Madame Bufferfly*

Italian composer
1858 – 1924

GIACOMO PUCCINI
Arranged by Richard Bradley

Un Bel Di - 2 - 1

HUNGARIAN RHAPSODY NO. 2

Hungarian pianist - composer
1811 – 1886

FRANZ LISZT
Arranged by Richard Bradley

WILLIAM TELL OVERTURE

Italian composer
1792 – 1868

GIOACCHINO ROSSINI
Arranged by Richard Bradley

with pedal

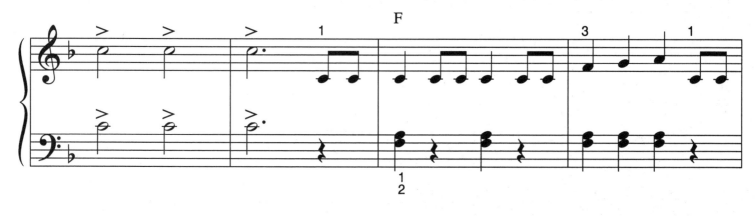

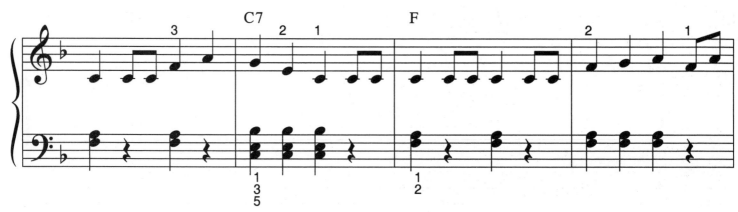

William Tell Overture - 4 - 1

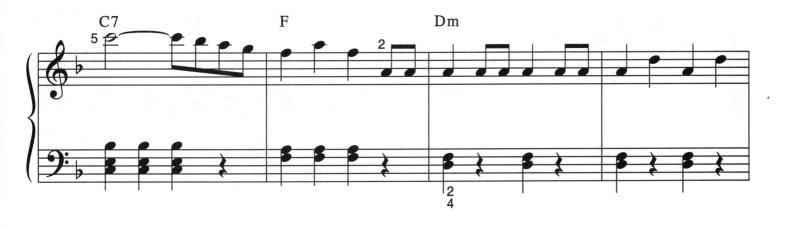

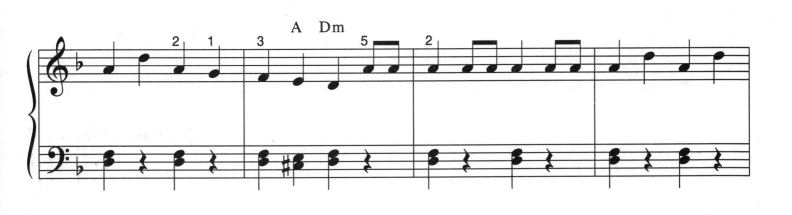

William Tell Overture - 4 - 2

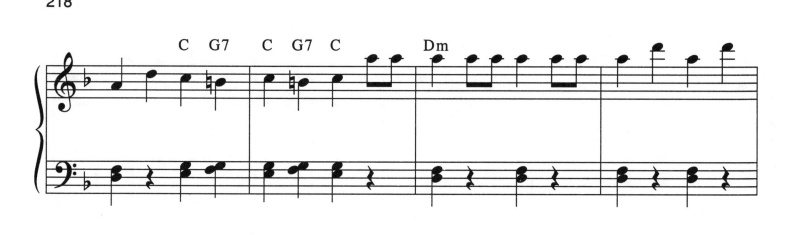

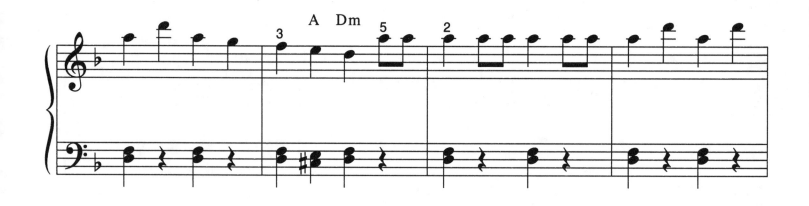

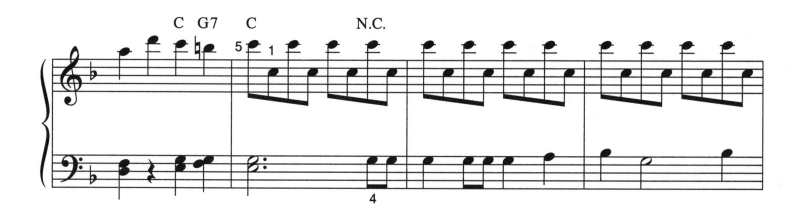

William Tell Overture - 4 - 4

PETER AND THE WOLF
(PETER'S THEME)

Russian composer
1891 – 1953

SERGEI PROKOFIEV
Arranged by Richard Bradley

Cheerful walking tempo ♩ = 96

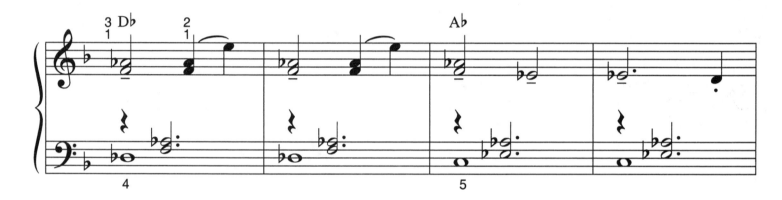

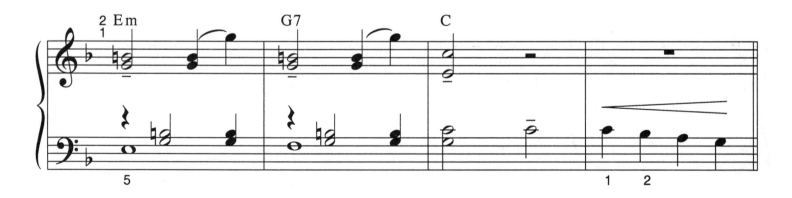

Peter and the Wolf - 2 - 1

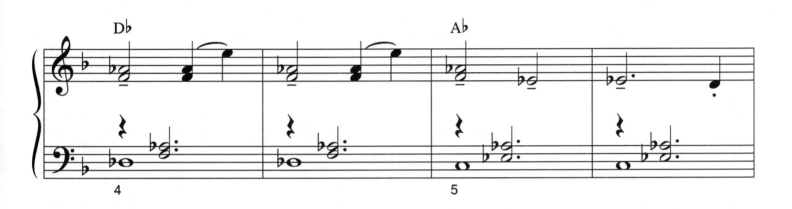

LULLABY

German composer
1833 – 1897

JOHANNES BRAHMS
Arranged by Richard Bradley

Lullaby - 2 - 1

Lullaby - 2 - 2

CLAIR DE LUNE
(FIRST THEME)

French composer
1862 – 1918

CLAUDE DEBUSSY
Arranged by Richard Bradley

Clair de Lune - 2 - 1

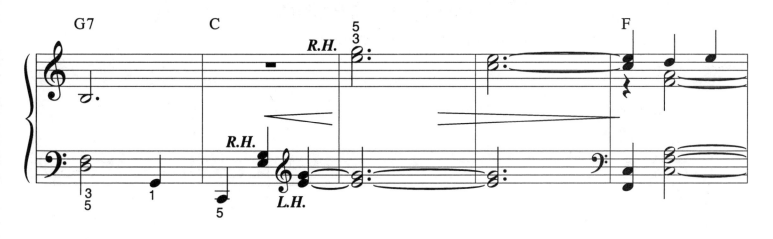

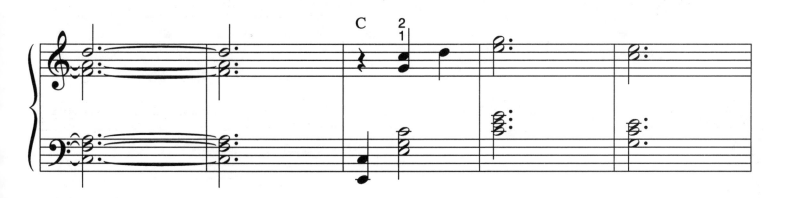

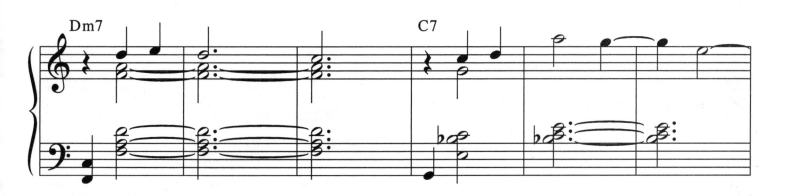

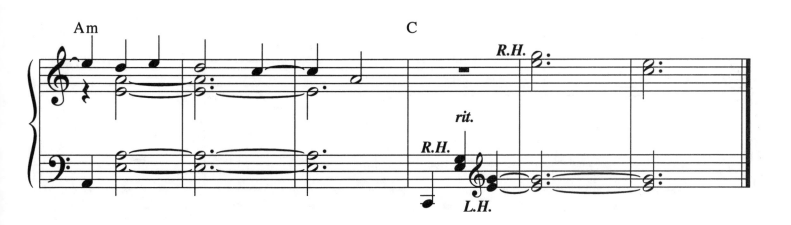

ALSO SPRACH ZARATHUSTRA

Used as the theme for the Motion Picture *2001: A Space Odyssey*

German composer
1864 – 1949

RICHARD STRAUSS
Arranged by Richard Bradley

FUNERAL MARCH OF THE MARIONETTES

Used as the theme for the TV series *Alfred Hitchcock Presents*

French composer
1818 – 1893

CHARLES GOUNOD
Arranged by Richard Bradley

Funeral March of the Marionettes - 2 - 1

Funeral March of the Marionettes - 2 - 2

THE WEST WING
(MAIN TITLE)

From the TV Series *The West Wing*

Composed by
W. G. SNUFFY WALDEN
Arranged by Richard Bradley

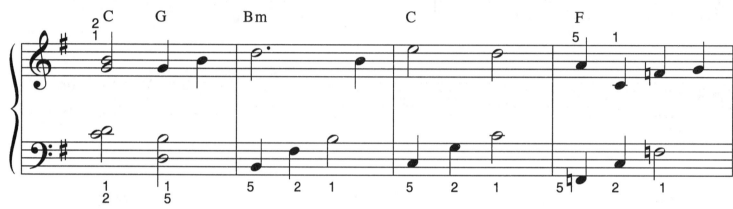

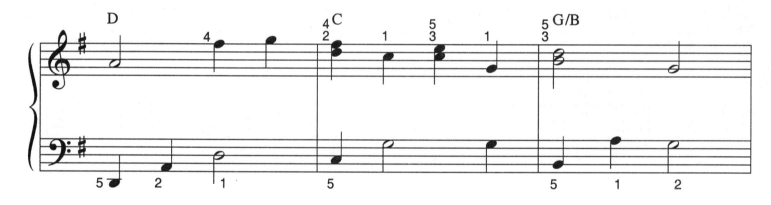

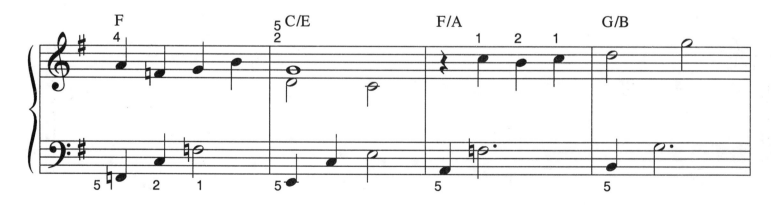

The West Wing - 2 - 1

BOSS OF ME

Theme from the TV Series *Malcolm in the Middle*
Recorded by They Might Be Giants

Words and Music by
JOHN FLANSBURGH
and JOHN LINNELL
Arranged by Richard Bradley

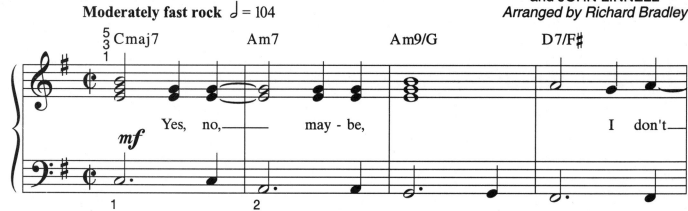

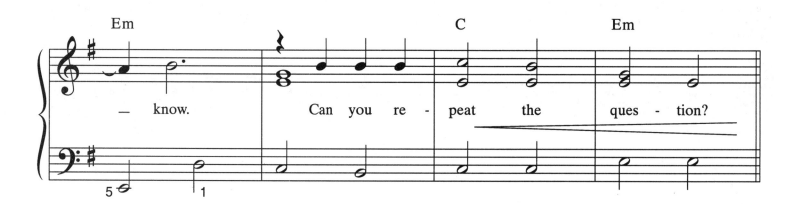

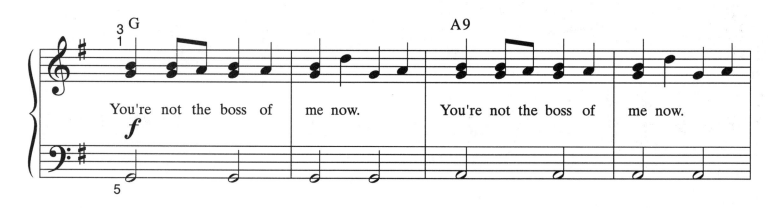

Boss of Me - 5 - 1

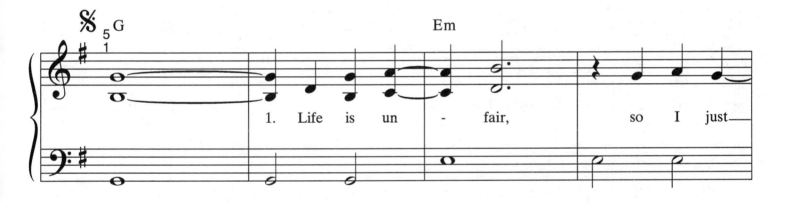

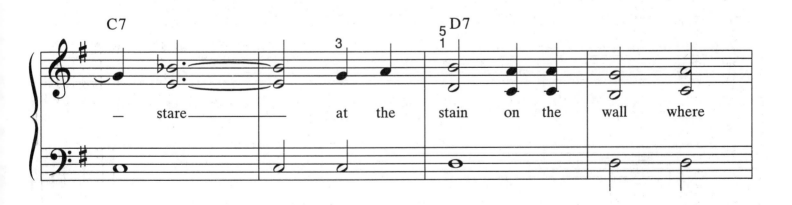

Boss of Me - 5 - 2

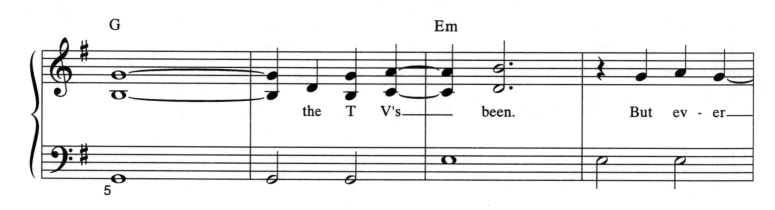

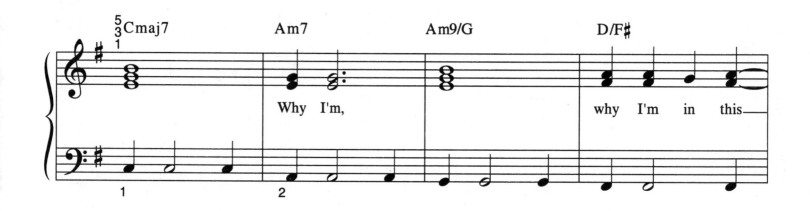

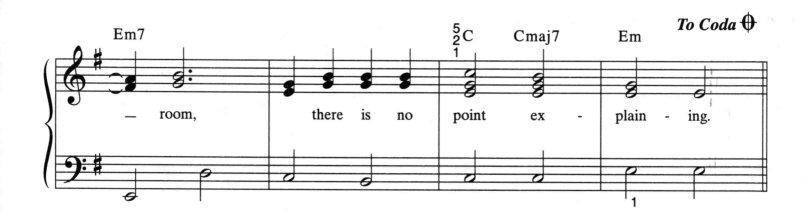

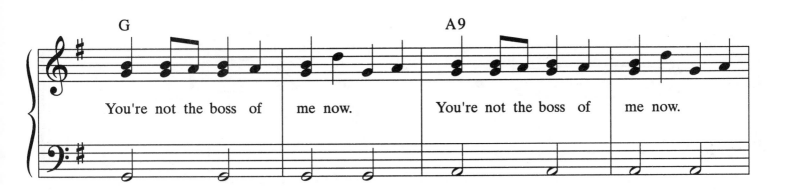

D.S. 𝄋 *al Coda* ⊕

Cmaj7   D5

You're not the boss of me now, and you're not so big.

G

Life is un - fair.

Verse 2:
Life is a test, but I confess
I like this mess I've made so far.
Grade on a curve, and you'll observe
I'm right below the horizon.
Yes, no, maybe, I don't know,
Can you repeat the question?

SONG FROM M*A*S*H

Theme from the Television Series *M*A*S*H*

Words and Music by
MIKE ALTMAN and JOHNNY MANDEL
Arranged by Richard Bradley

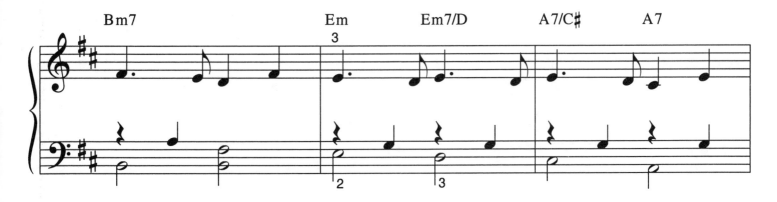

Song from M*A*S*H - 3 - 1

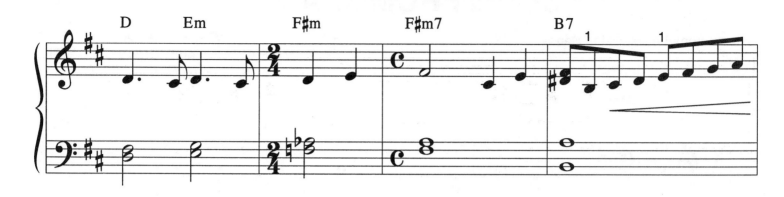

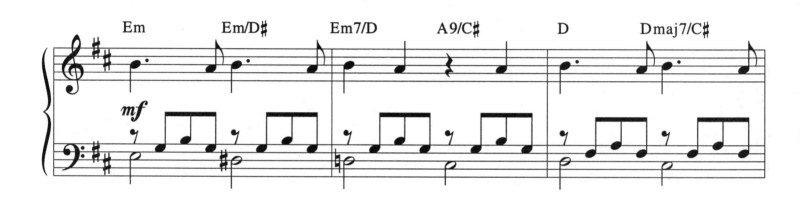

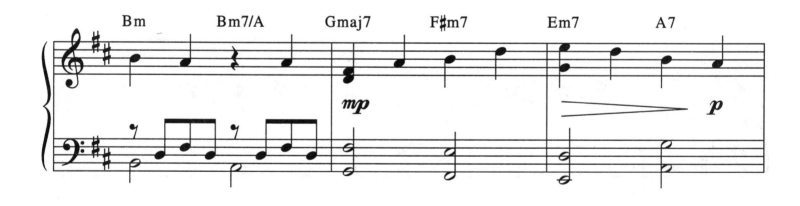

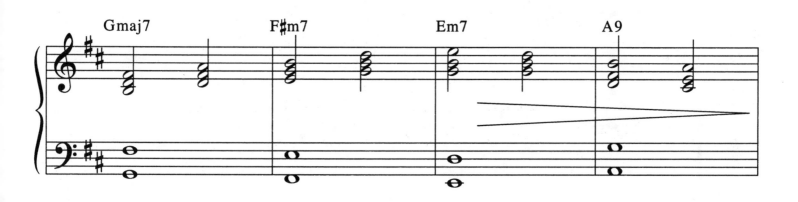

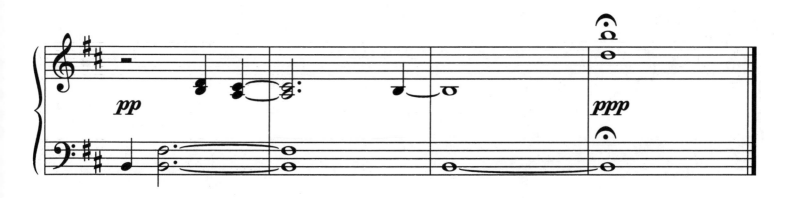

I'LL BE THERE FOR YOU

Theme from the TV Series *Friends*
Recorded by The Rembrandts

Words by DAVID CRANE, MARTA KAUFMAN,
PHIL SOLEM, DANNY WILDE and ALLEE WILLIS
Music by MICHAEL SKLOFF
Arranged by Richard Bradley

So, no — one told you life — was gon-na be — this way.

Your job's — a joke, you're broke, — your love life's D. O. A.

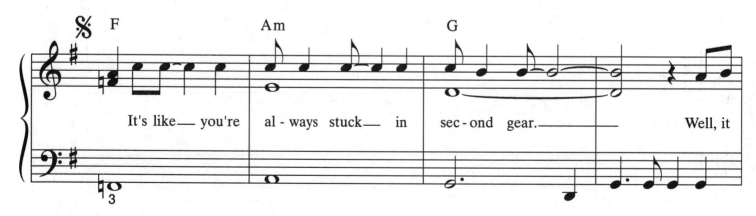

It's like — you're al - ways stuck — in sec - ond gear. — Well, it

I'll Be There for You - 6 - 1

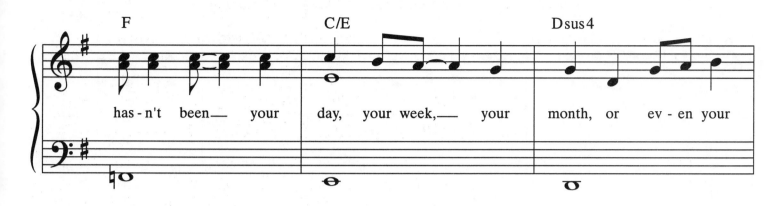

has - n't been— your day, your week,— your month, or ev - en your

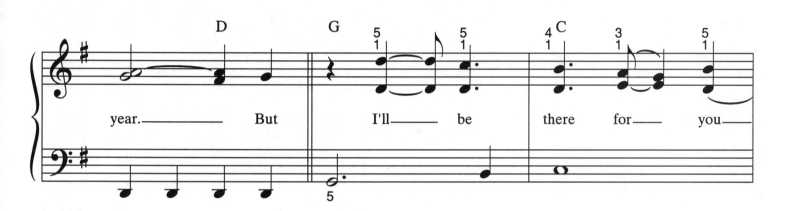

year.———— But I'll—— be there for—— you—

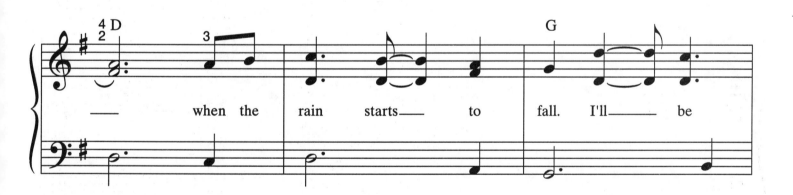

— when the rain starts—— to fall. I'll—— be

there for—— you—— like I've been there—— be -

To Coda

fore. I'll— be | there for— you— | 'cause you're | there for— me,

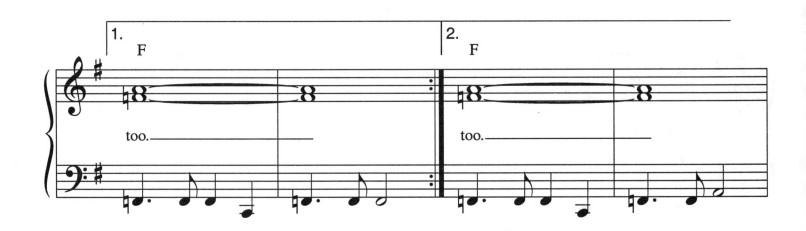

1. | 2.

too.— | too.—

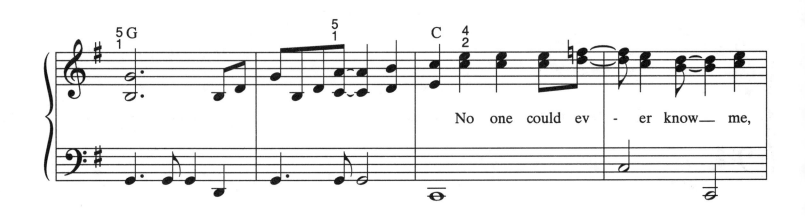

No one could ev - er know— me,

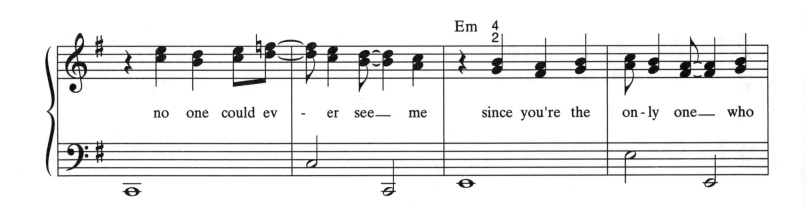

no one could ev - er see— me | since you're the | on-ly one— who

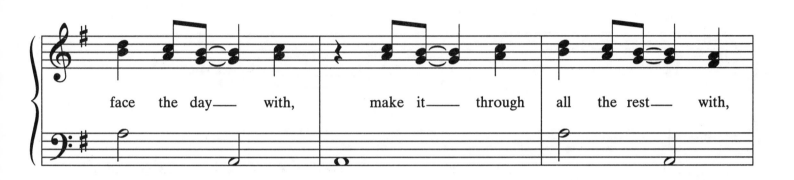

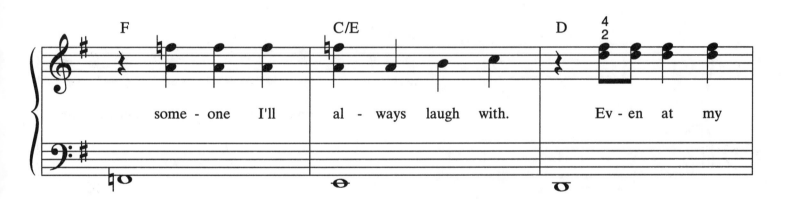

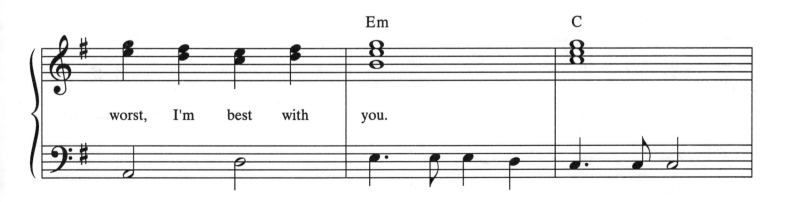

I'll Be There for You - 6 - 4

244

D.S. 𝄋 al Coda ⊕

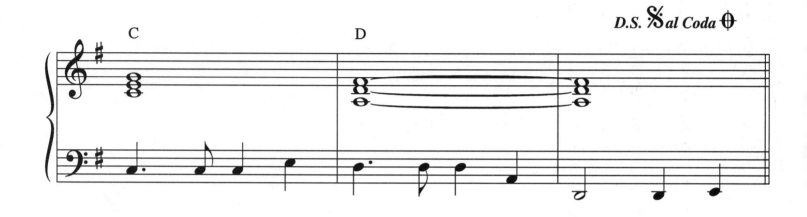

too._____ I'll____ be there for____ you

when the rain starts____ to fall. I'll____ be

there   for____ you____   like I've   been   there____   be -

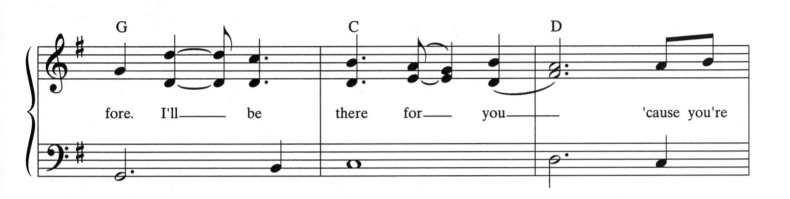

fore.   I'll____   be   there   for____ you____   'cause you're

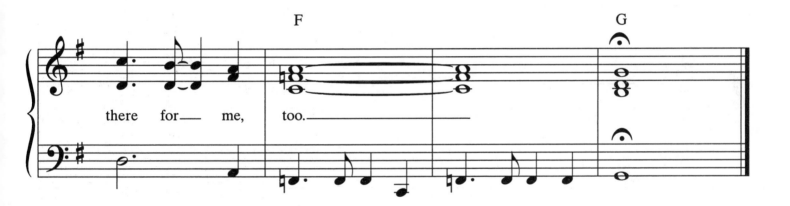

there   for____ me,   too.____

Verse 2:
You're still in bed at ten and work began at eight.
You've burned your breakfast, so far, everything is great.
Your mother warned you there'd be days like these,
But she didn't tell you when the world has brought you down to your knees, that
(To Chorus:)

THEME FROM "NYPD BLUE"

From the TV Series *NYPD Blue*

Music by
MIKE POST
Arranged by Richard Bradley

Moderately fast $\quad \textbf{\textit{♩}} = 198$

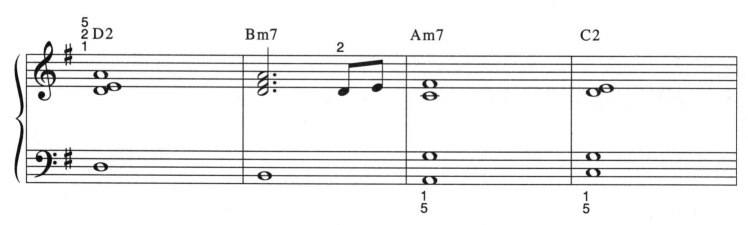

Theme from "NYPD Blue" - 2 - 1

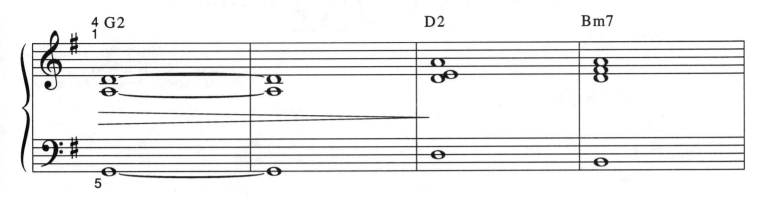

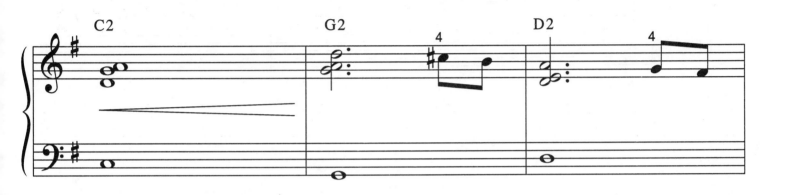

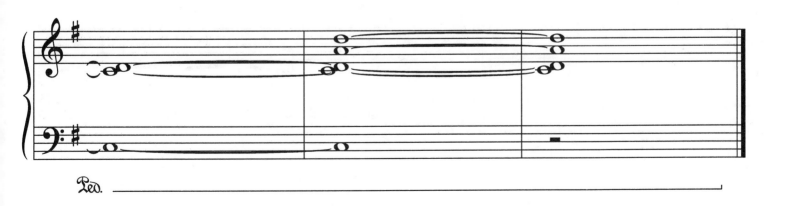

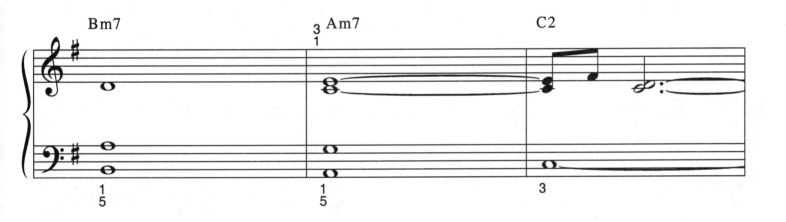

Theme from "NYPD Blue" - 2 - 2

THEME FROM
"THE X-FILES"

From the TV Series *The X-Files*

Music by
MARK SNOW
Arranged by Richard Bradley

with pedal

Theme from "The X-Files" - 6 - 1

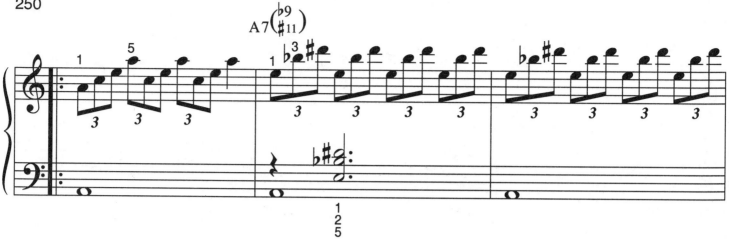

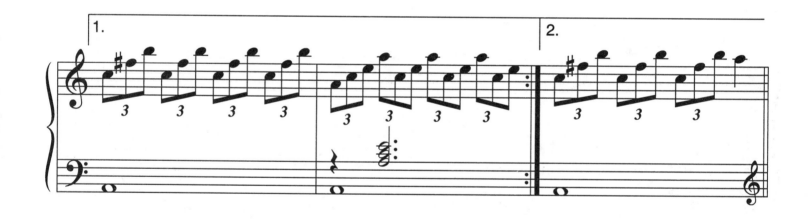

Theme from "The X-Files" - 6 - 3

JEOPARDY THEME

From the TV Series *Jeopardy*

Music by
MERV GRIFFIN
Arranged by Richard Bradley

Moderately bright ♩ = 116

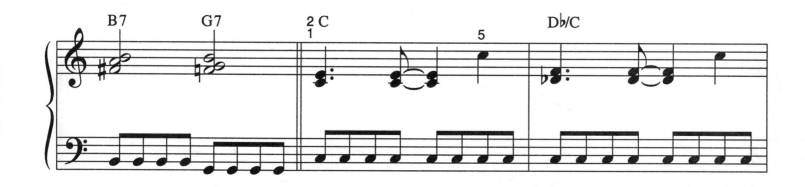

Jeopardy Theme - 2 - 1

Jeopardy Theme - 2 - 2

255

CHANGING KEYS
(WHEEL OF FORTUNE THEME)

From the TV Series *Wheel of Fortune*

By MERV GRIFFIN
Arranged by Richard Bradley

Changing Keys - 4 - 1

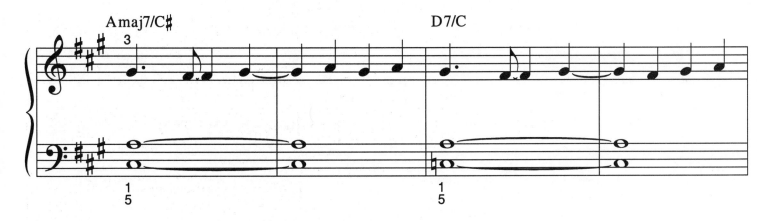

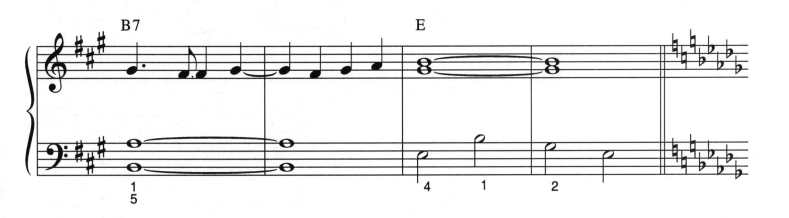

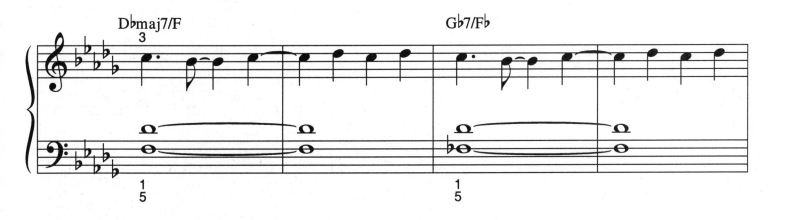

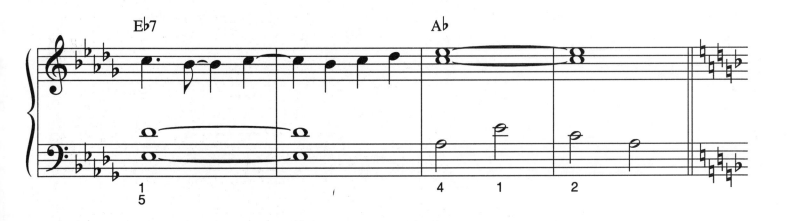

Changing Keys - 4 - 2

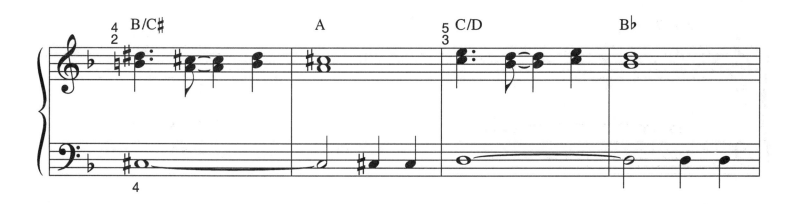

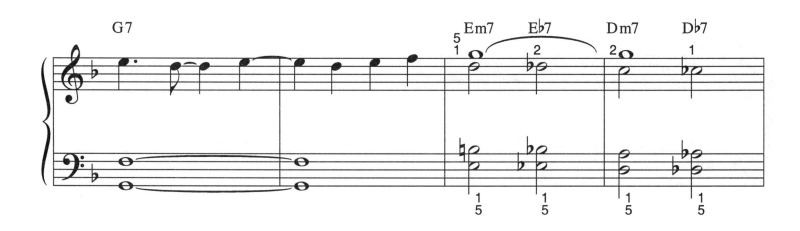

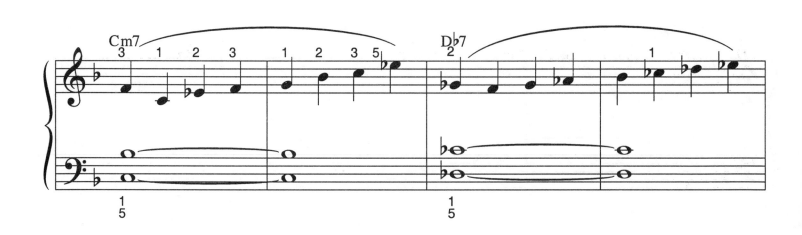

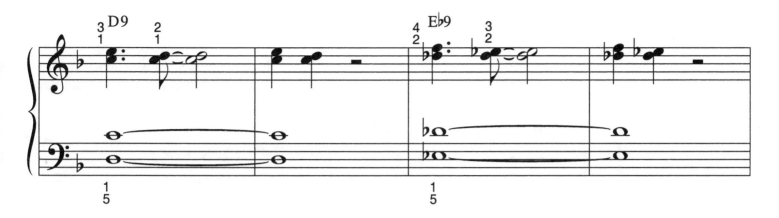

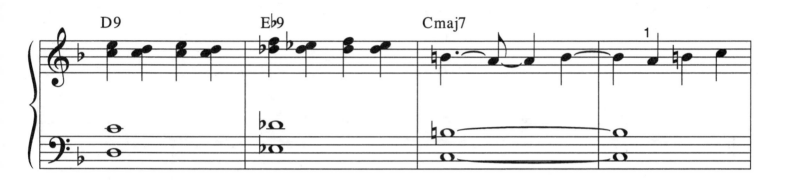

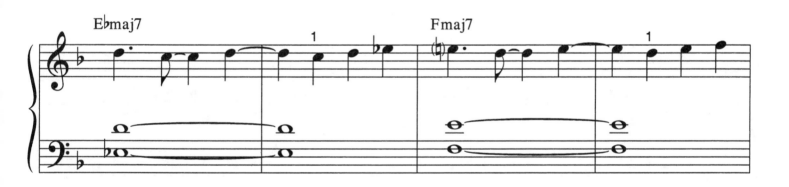

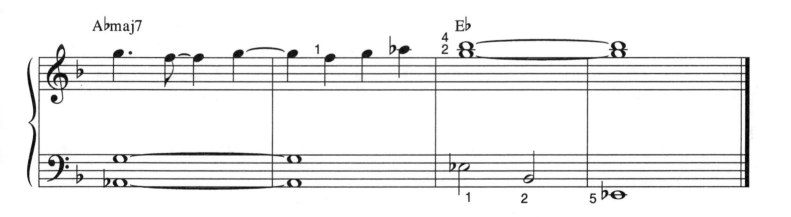

Changing Keys - 4 - 4

ER
(MAIN THEME)

From the TV Series *ER*

Composed by
JAMES NEWTON HOWARD
Arranged by Richard Bradley

ER - 2 - 1

KING OF THE HILL

From the Twentieth Century Fox TV Series *King Of The Hill*

Words and Music by
ROGER CLYNE, BRIAN BLUSH,
ARTHUR EDWARDS and PAUL NAFFAH
Arranged by Richard Bradley

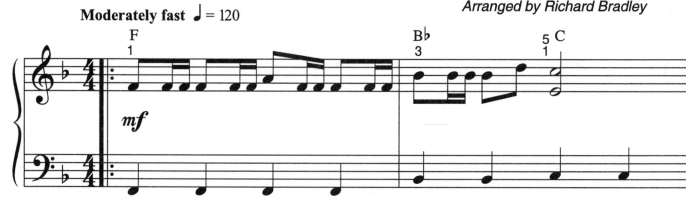

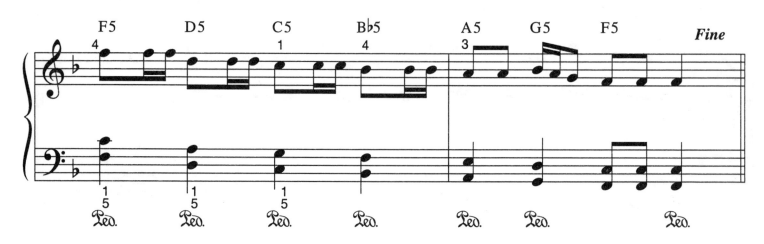

King of the Hill - 2 - 1

EVERYBODY LOVES RAYMOND
(MAIN TITLE)

From the TV Series *Everybody Loves Raymond*

Words and Music by
RICK MAROTTA
and TERRY TROTTER
Arranged by Richard Bradley

THE THEME FROM
"THE ANDY GRIFFITH SHOW"
("THE FISHIN' HOLE")

From the TV Series *The Andy Griffith Show*

Lyric by EVERETT SLOANE
Music by EARLE HAGEN and HERBERT SPENCER
Arranged by Richard Bradley

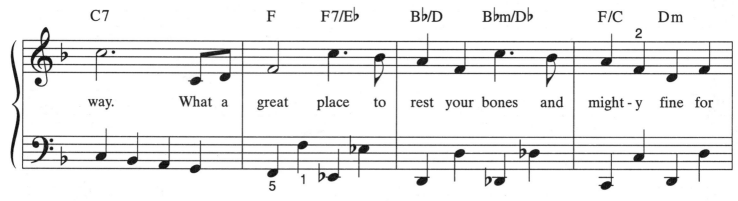

The Theme from "The Andy Griffith Show" - 2 - 1

THE BALLAD OF GILLIGAN'S ISLE

Theme from the TV Series *Gilligan's Island*

Words and Music by
SHERWOOD SCHWARTZ
and GEORGE WYLE
Arranged by Richard Bradley

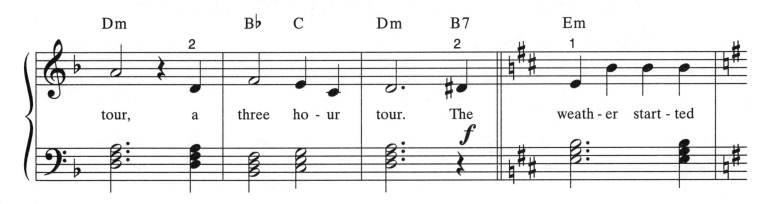

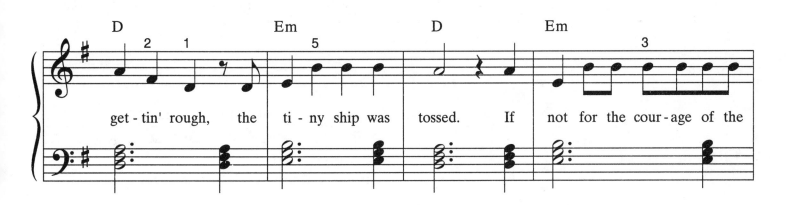

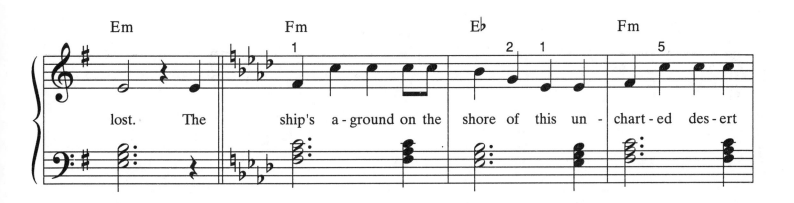

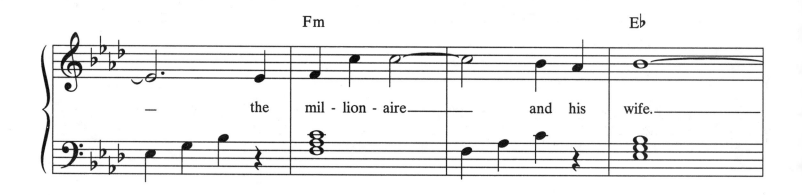

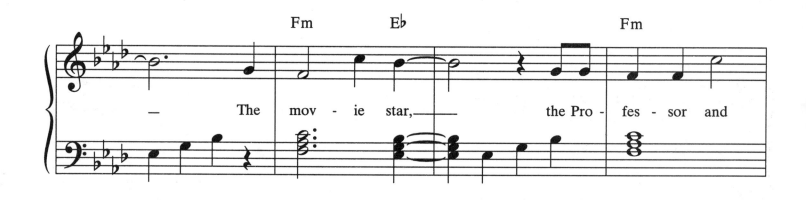

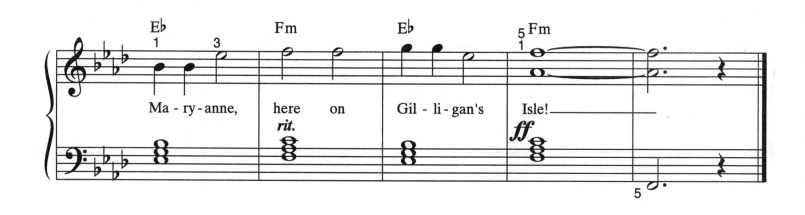

GOD BLESS THE U.S.A.

Recorded by Lee Greenwood

Words and Music by
LEE GREENWOOD
Arranged by Richard Bradley

God Bless the U.S.A. - 5 - 1

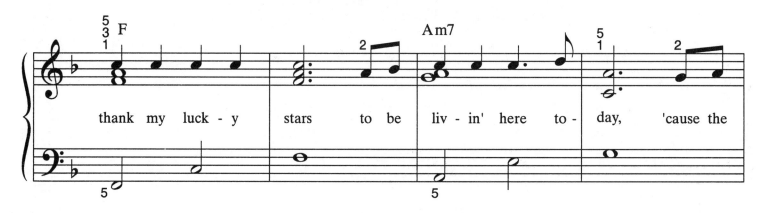

thank my luck - y stars to be liv - in' here to - day, 'cause the

flag still stands for free - dom and they can't take that a -

way. And I'm proud to be an A -

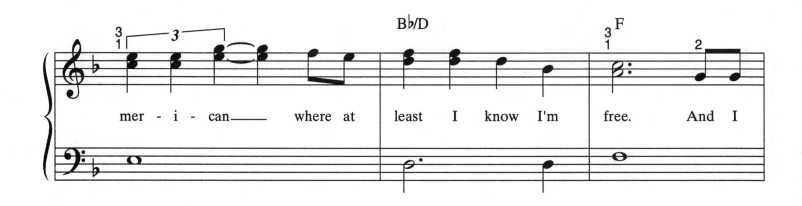

mer - i - can where at least I know I'm free. And I

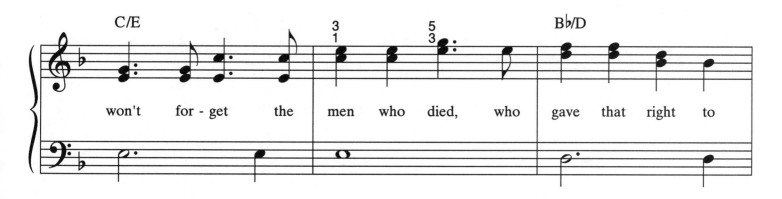

C/E ... Bb/D

won't for-get the men who died, who gave that right to

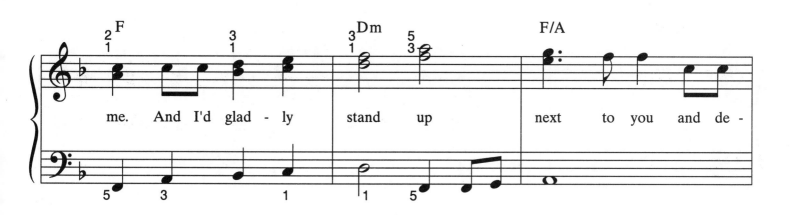

F ... Dm ... F/A

me. And I'd glad-ly stand up next to you and de-

Bb ... Am7 ... Gm7 ... F/A

fend her still to-day, 'cause there ain't no doubt I love this land,___

To Coda ⊕   Bb   C11   F   Am7/E

— God bless the U. S. A.

God Bless the U.S.A. - 5 - 3

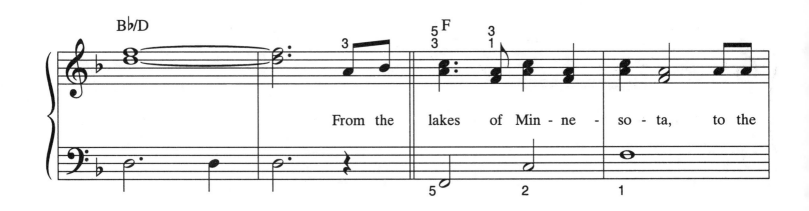

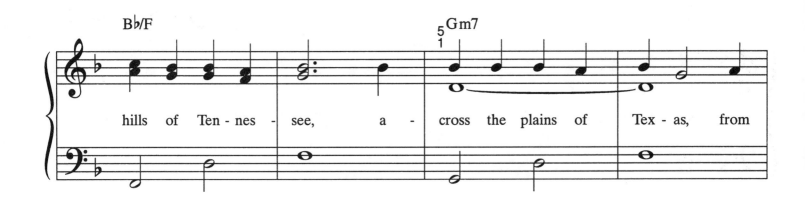

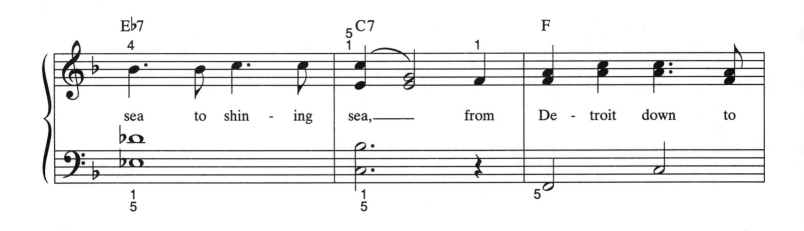

Hous - ton and New York to L. A. well, there's

pride in ev - 'ry A - mer - i - can heart, and it's time to stand and

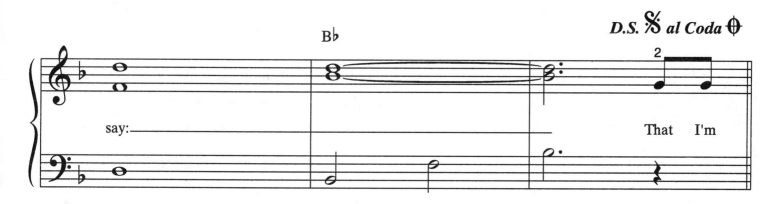

D.S. 𝄋 al Coda 𝄌

say:_____ That I'm

Coda

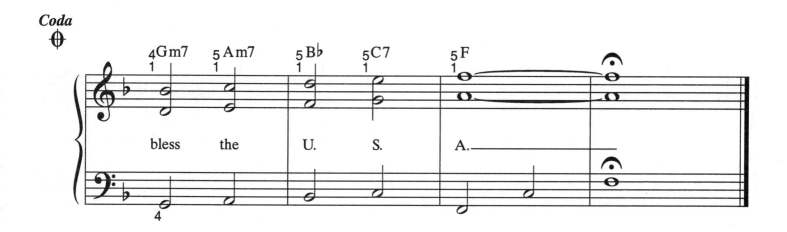

bless the U. S. A._____

ANCHORS AWEIGH

Words and Music by
Captain ALFRED H. MILES U.S.N. (RET.),
CHARLES A. ZIMMERMAN and GEORGE D. LOTTMAN
Arranged by Richard Bradley

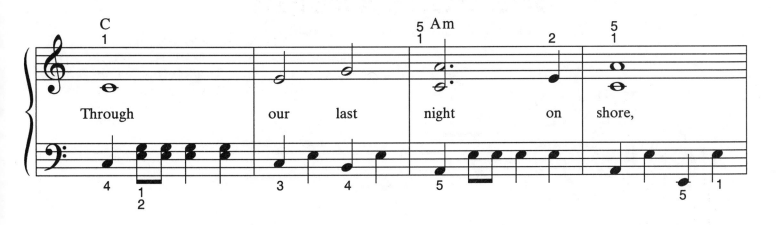

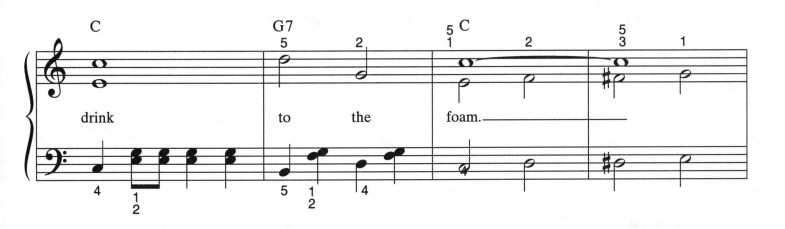

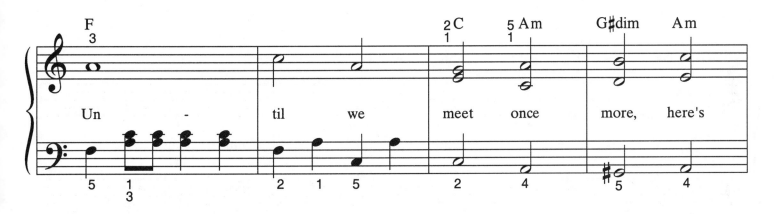

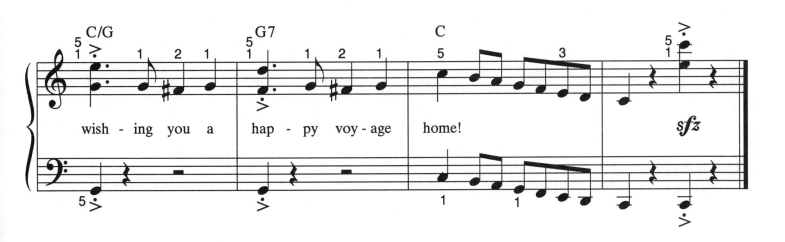

THE U.S. AIR FORCE
(THE WILD BLUE YONDER)

Words and Music by
ROBERT CRAWFORD
Arranged by Richard Bradley

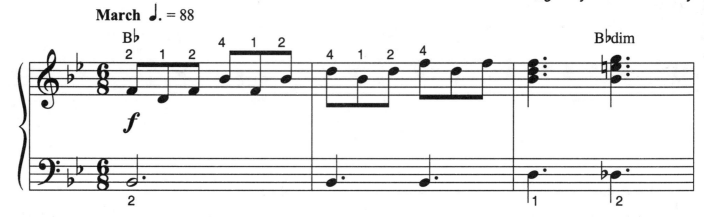

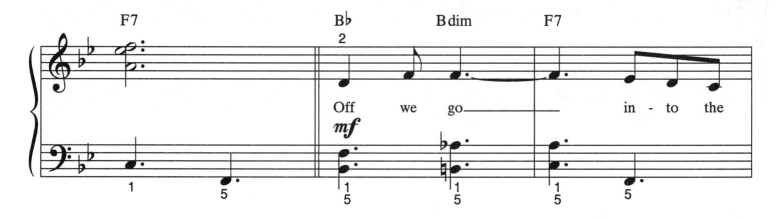

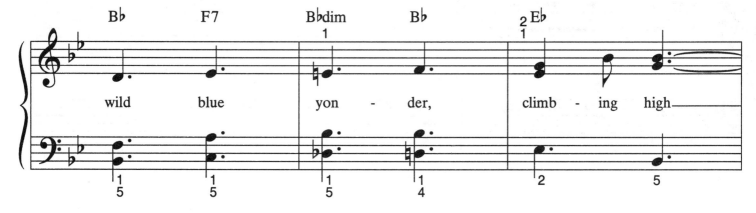

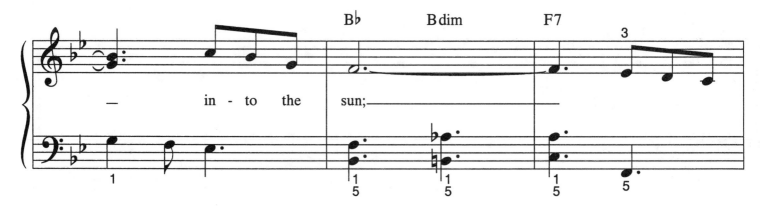

The U.S. Air Force - 3 - 1

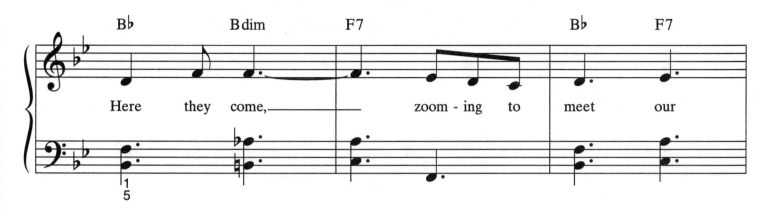

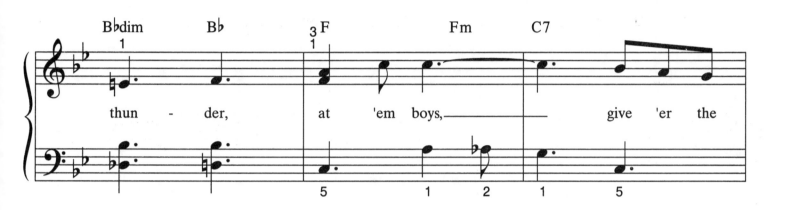

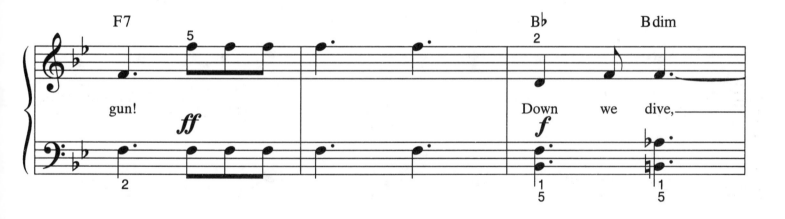

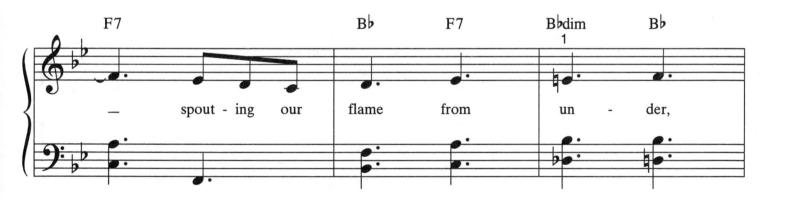

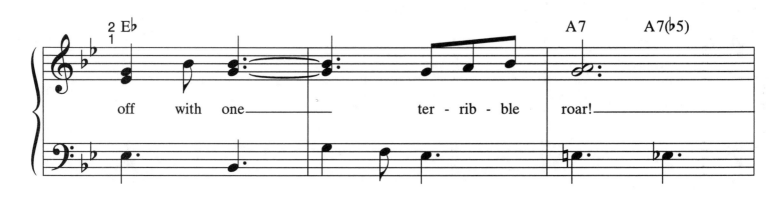

off with one_____ ter - rib - ble roar!_____

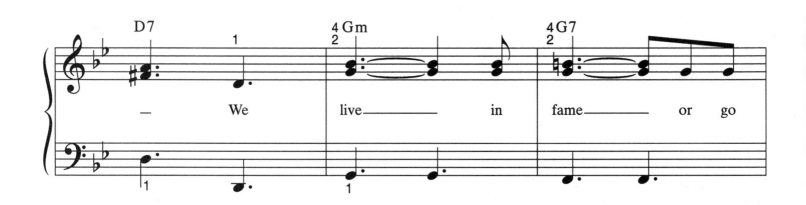

_____ We live_____ in fame_____ or go

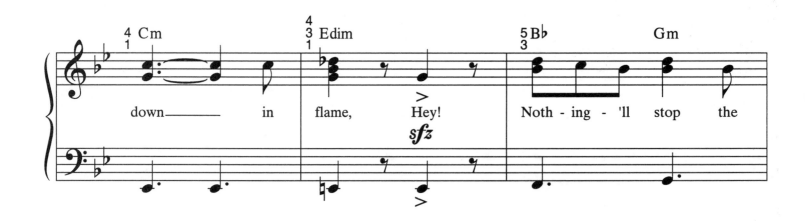

down_____ in flame, Hey! Noth - ing - 'll stop the

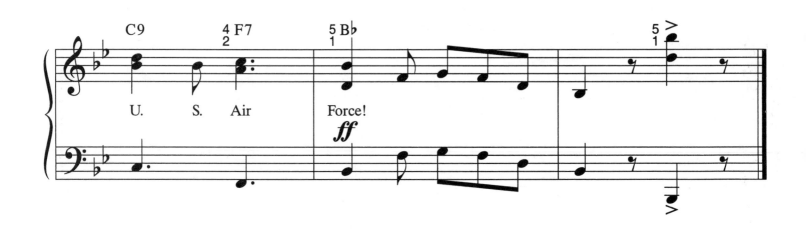

U. S. Air Force!

THE MARINES HYMN
(FROM THE HALLS OF MONTEZUMA)

Words by L. Z. PHILLIPS
Music based on a theme by JACQUES OFFENBACH
Arranged by Richard Bradley

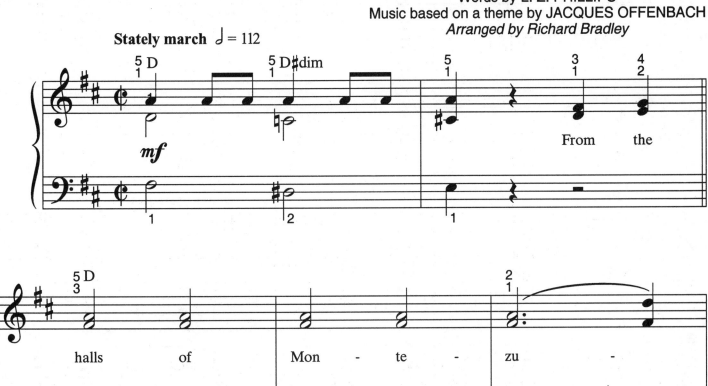

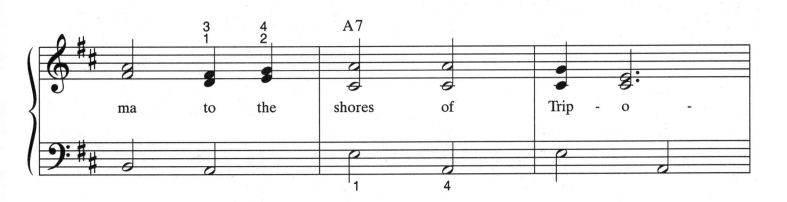

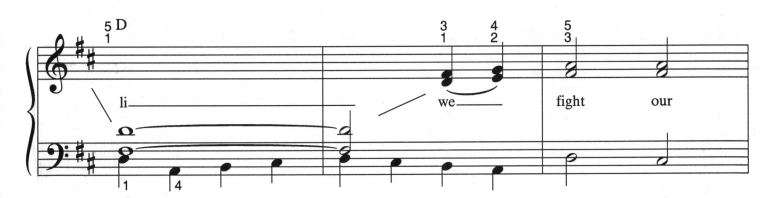

The Marines Hymn - 3 - 1

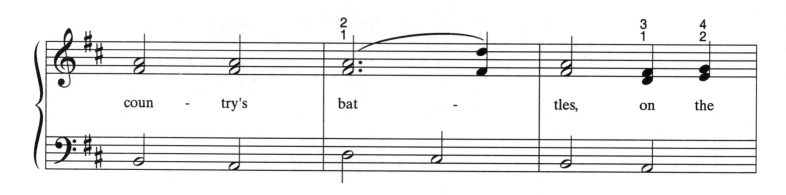

coun - try's bat - tles, on the

land as on the sea.

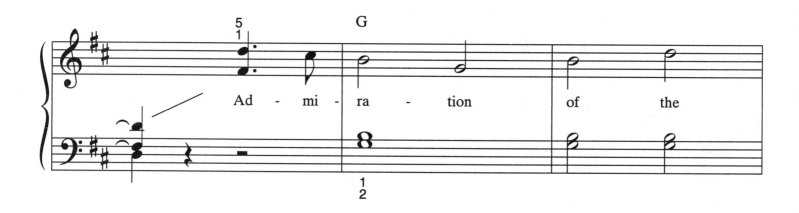

Ad - mi - ra - tion of the

na - tion, we're the fin - est

THE CAISSONS GO ROLLING ALONG
(U.S. FIELD ARTILLERY SONG)

By EDMUND L. GRUBER
Arranged by Richard Bradley

Bright march ♩ = 98

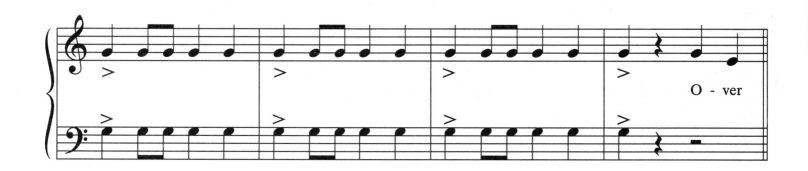

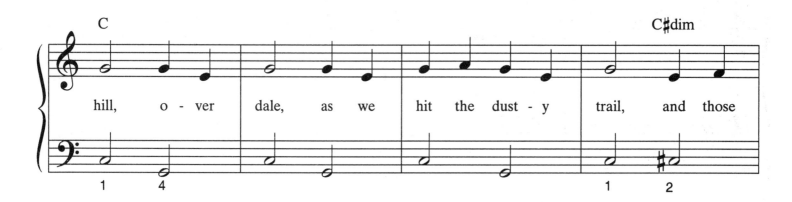

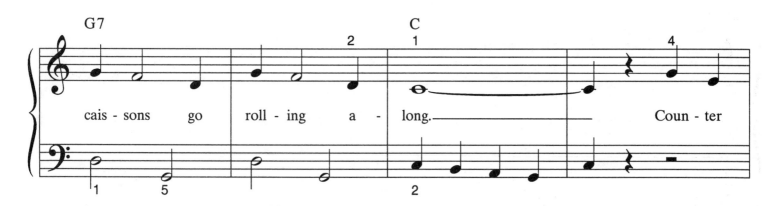

The Caissons Go Rolling Along - 3 - 1

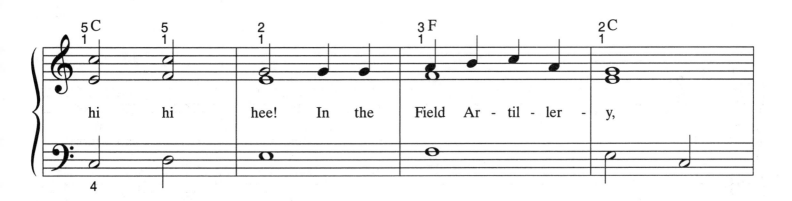

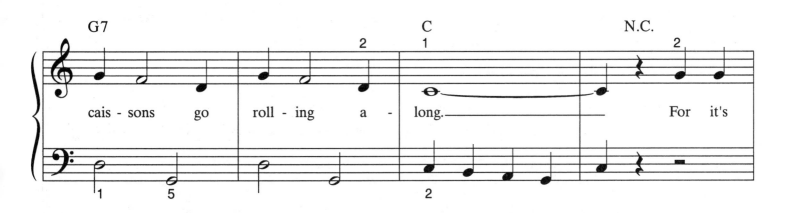

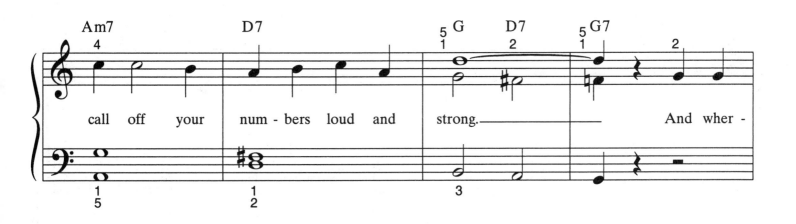

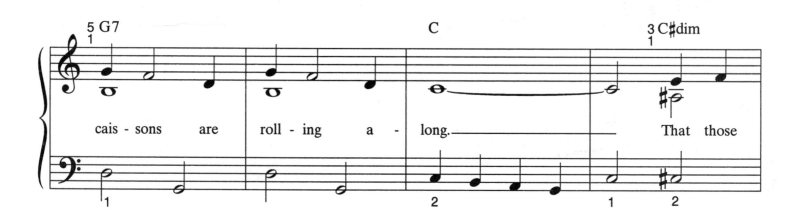

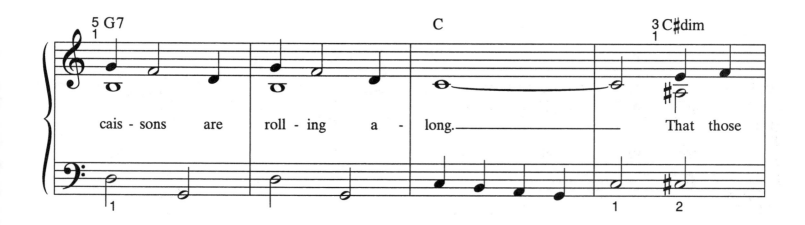

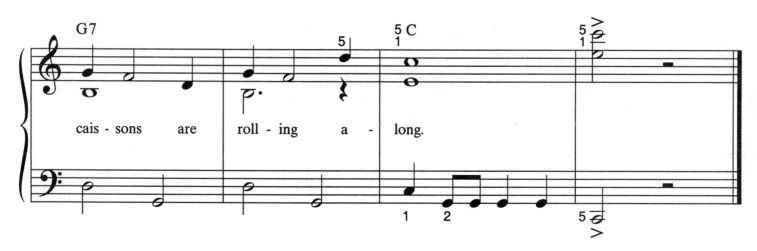

The Caissons Go Rolling Along - 3 - 3

YOU'RE A GRAND OLD FLAG

Words and Music by
GEORGE M. COHAN
Arranged by Richard Bradley

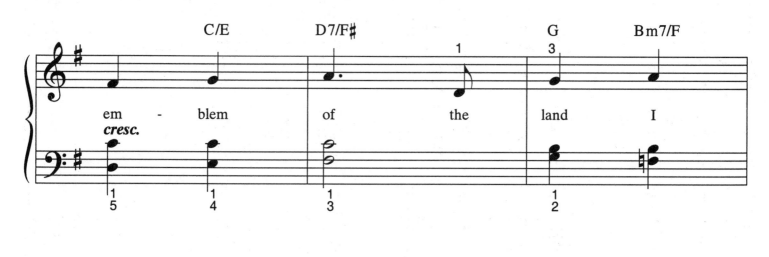

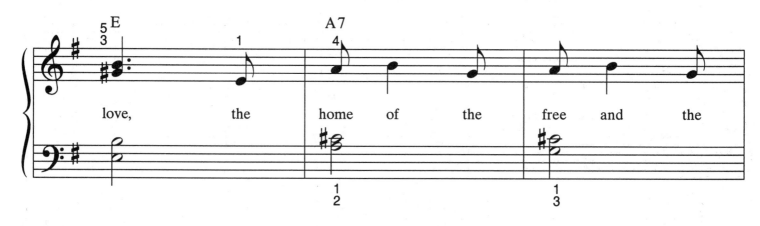

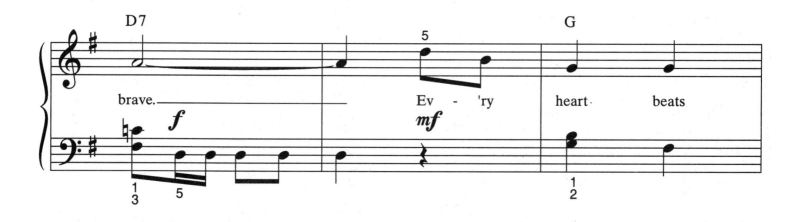

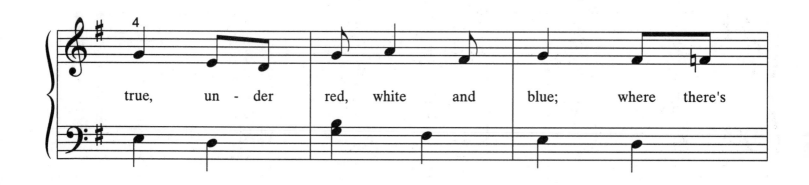

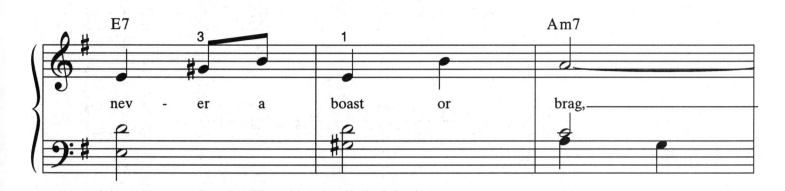

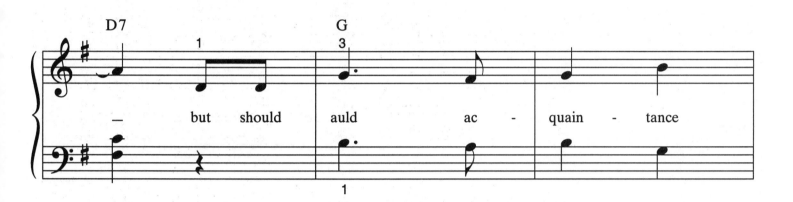

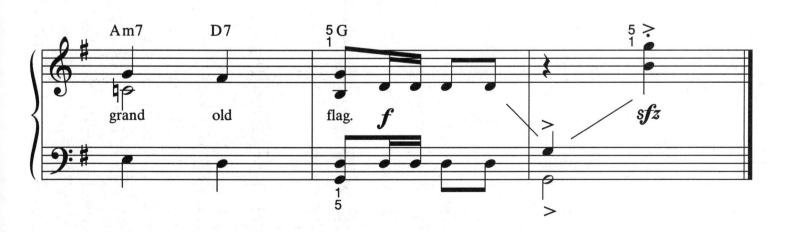

THE STARS AND STRIPES FOREVER

By JOHN PHILIP SOUSA
Arranged by Richard Bradley

The Stars and Stripes Forever - 4 - 1

The Stars and Stripes Forever - 4 - 2

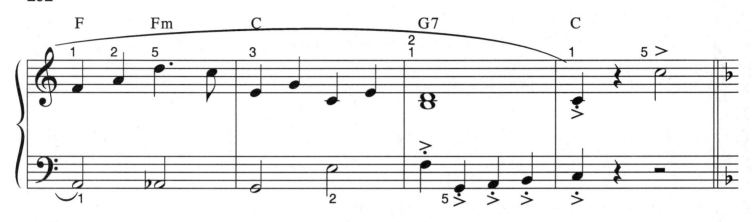

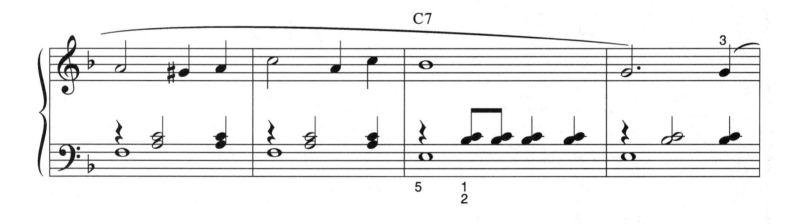

The Stars and Stripes Forever - 4 - 3

The Stars and Stripes Forever - 4 - 4

AMERICA
(MY COUNTRY TIS OF THEE)

Words by SAMUEL F. SMITH
TRADITIONAL MELODY
Arranged by Richard Bradley

Majestically ♩ = 88

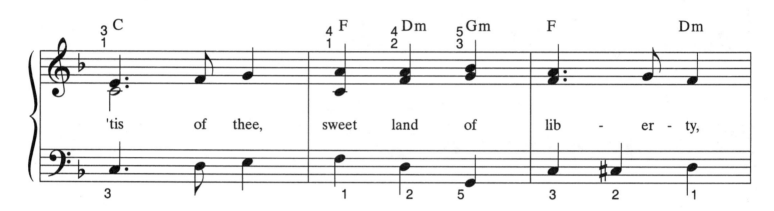

My coun - try 'tis of thee, sweet land of lib - er - ty,

of thee I sing. Land where my

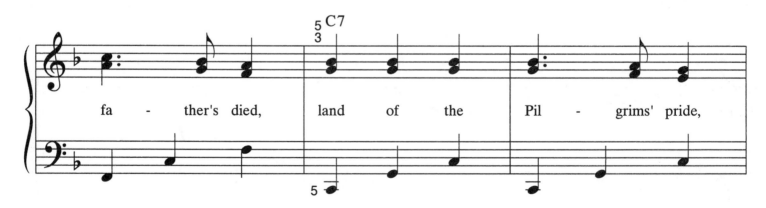

fa - ther's died, land of the Pil - grims' pride,

YANKEE DOODLE

TRADITIONAL
Arranged by Richard Bradley

Yan - kee Doo - dle keep it up, Yan - kee Doo - dle

Dan - dy, mind the mu - sic and the step, and

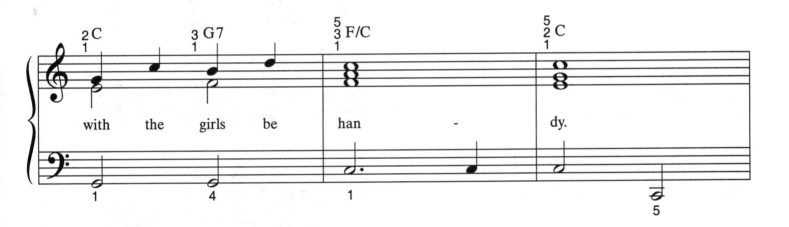

with the girls be han - dy.

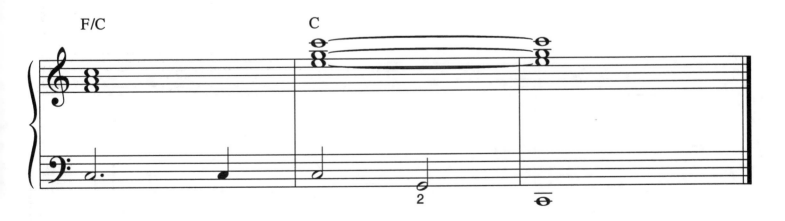

THE BATTLE HYMN OF THE REPUBLIC

Words by JULIA WARD HOWE
Music by WILLIAM STEFFE
Arranged by Richard Bradley

Moderate march ♩ = 96

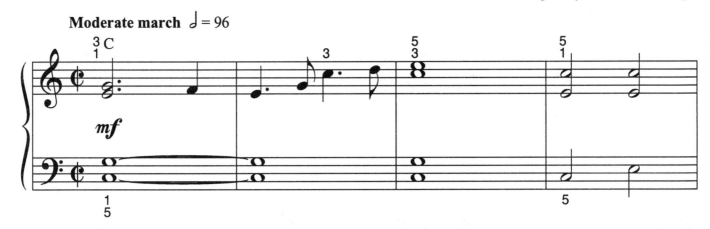

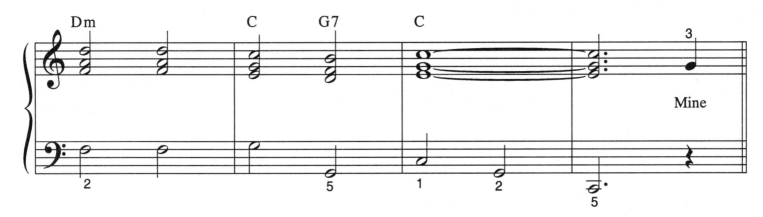

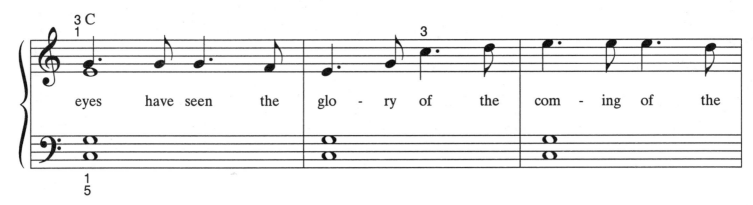

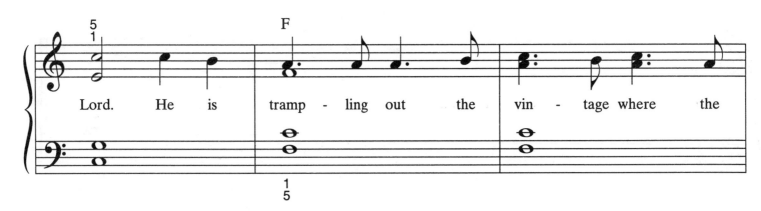

The Battle Hymn of the Republic - 3 - 1

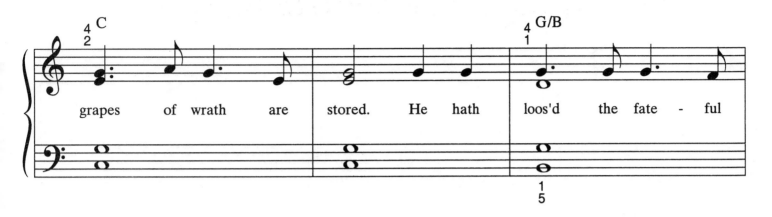

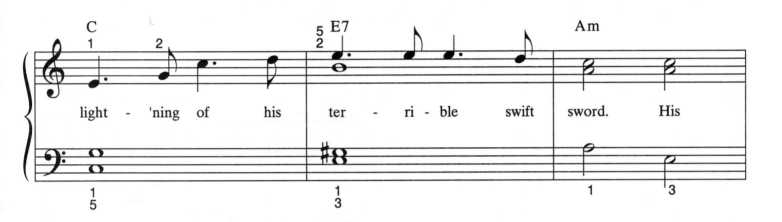

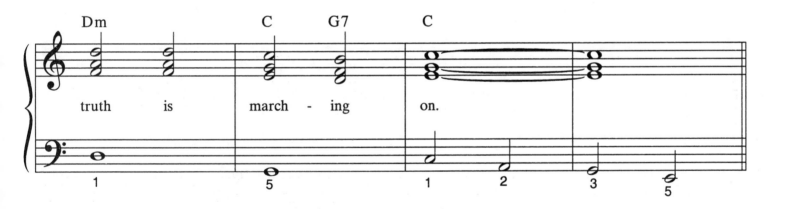

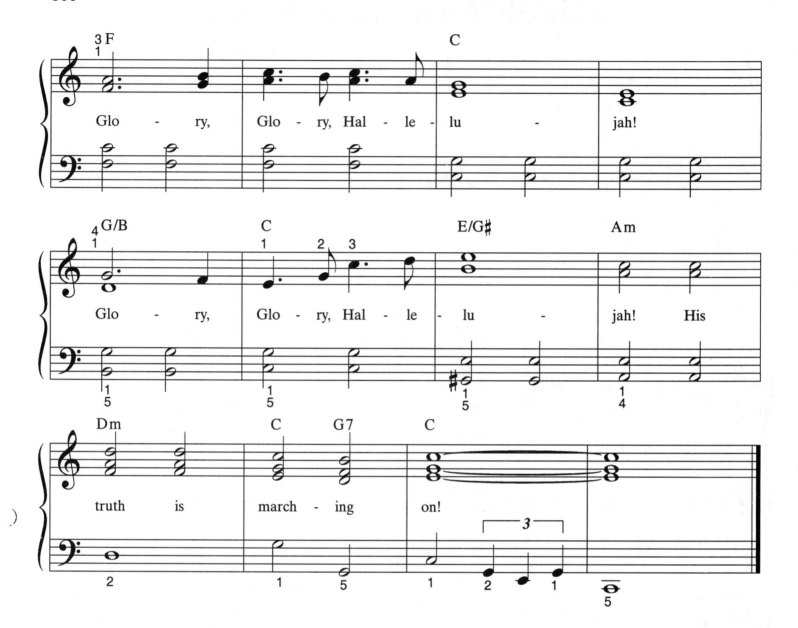

Additional Lyrics:

2. I have seen Him in the watch-fires of a hundred circling camps.
They have builded Him an alter in the evening dews and damps.
I have read his righteous sentence by the dim and flaring lamps.
His day is marching on.
(Chorus:)

3. I have read a fiery gospel writ in burnished rows of seel,
"As ye deal with my contempters, so with you my grace shall deal."
Let the hero born of woman crush the serpent with his heel,
Since God is marching on.
(Chorus:)

4. He has sounded forth the trumpet that shall never call retreat.
He is sifting out the hearts of men before His judgement seat.
O be swift, my soul, to answer Him, be jubilant my feet,
Our God is marching on.
(Chorus:)

AMERICA THE BEAUTIFUL

Words by KATHERINE LEE BATES
Music by SAMUEL A. WARD
Arranged by Richard Bradley

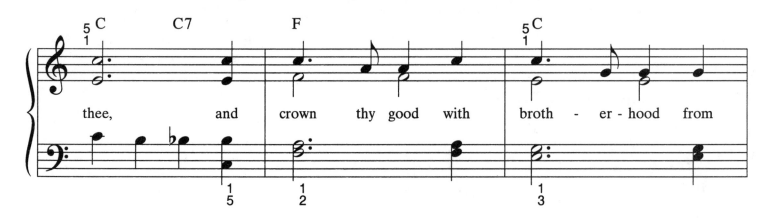

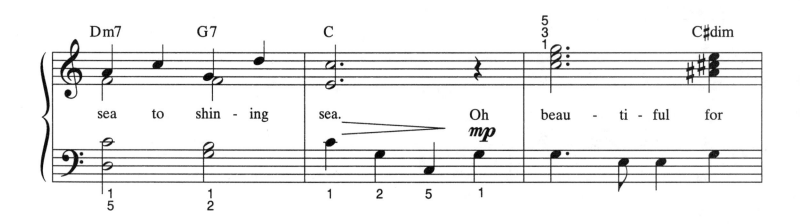

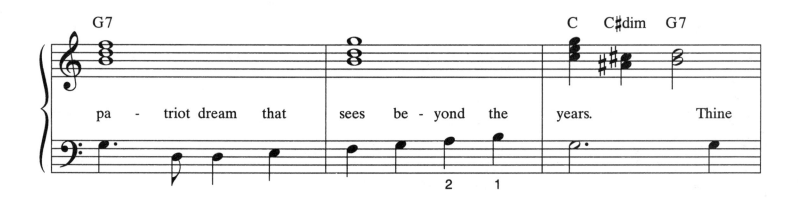

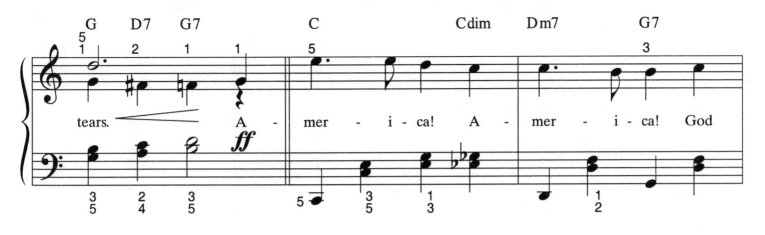

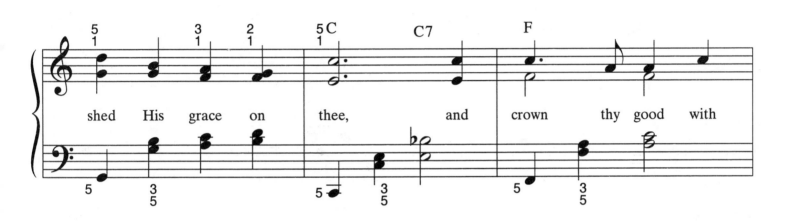

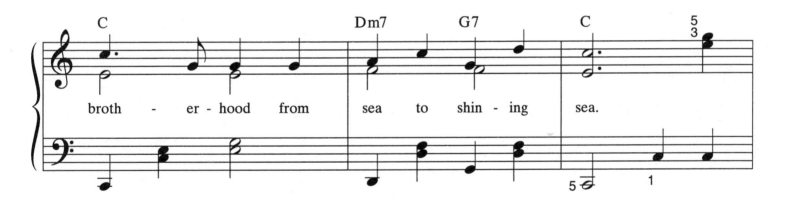

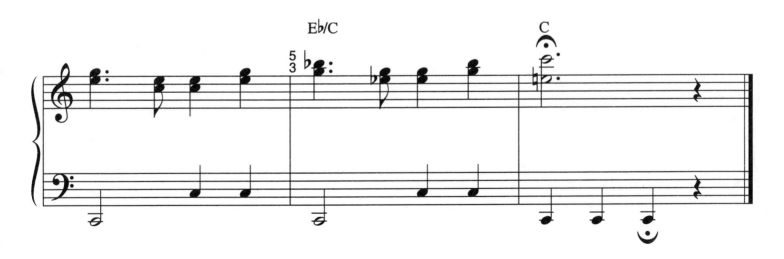

THE STAR-SPANGLED BANNER

Words by FRANCIS SCOTT KEY
Music by JOHN STAFFORD SMITH
Arranged by Richard Bradley

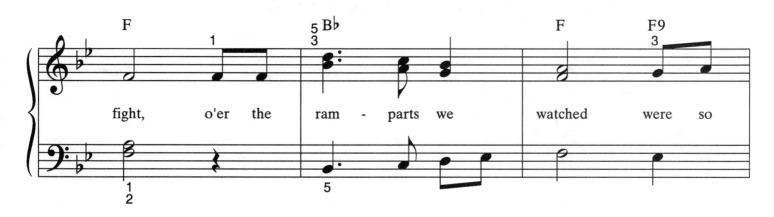

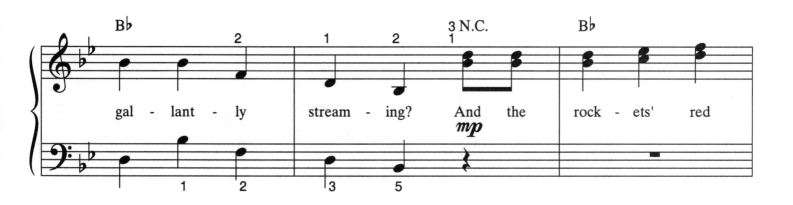

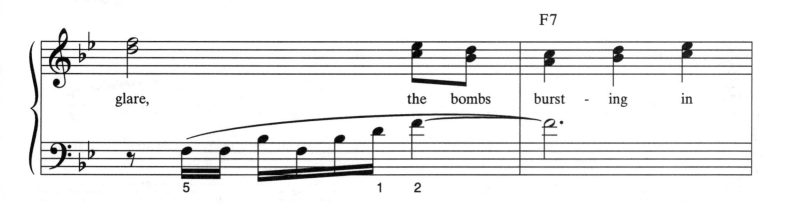

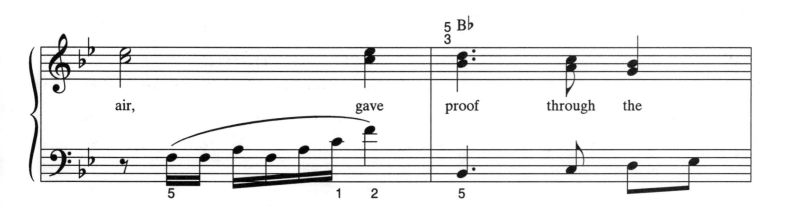

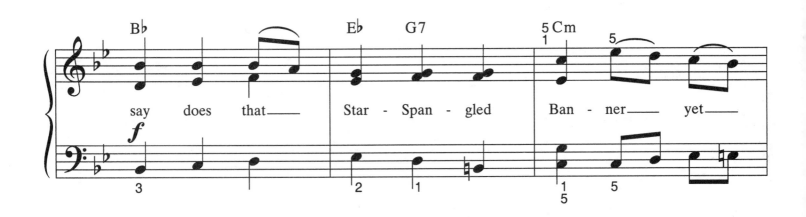

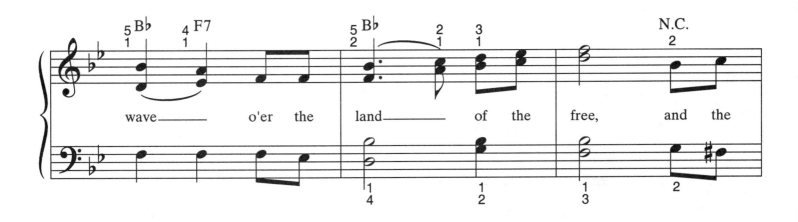

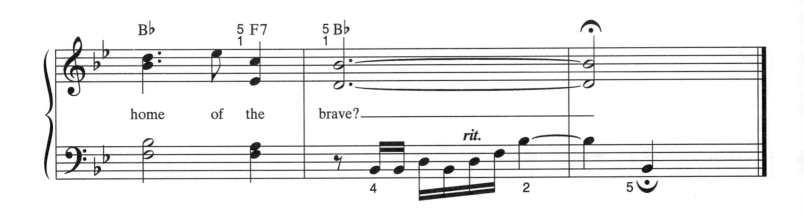

ALL THE THINGS YOU ARE

From the Broadway Musical *Very Warm for May*

Words by OSCAR HAMMERSTEIN II
Music by JEROME KERN
Arranged by Richard Bradley

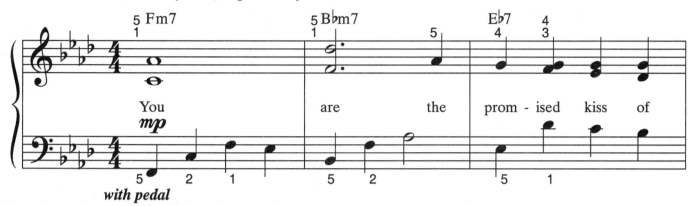

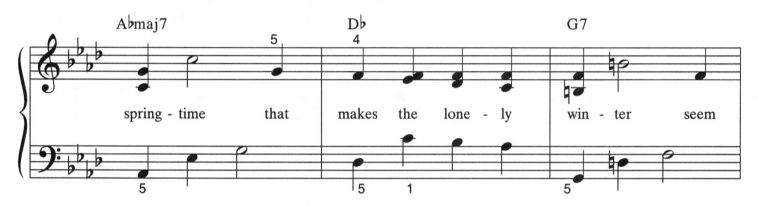

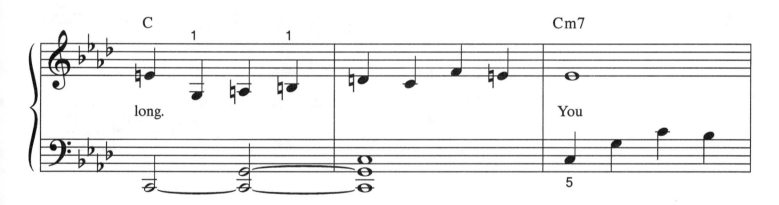

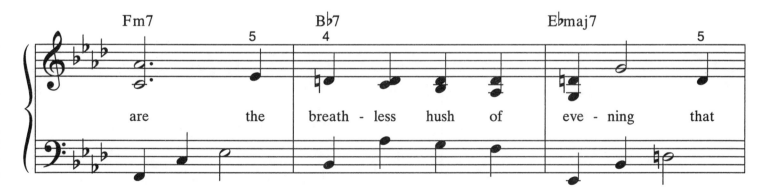

All the Things You Are - 3 - 1

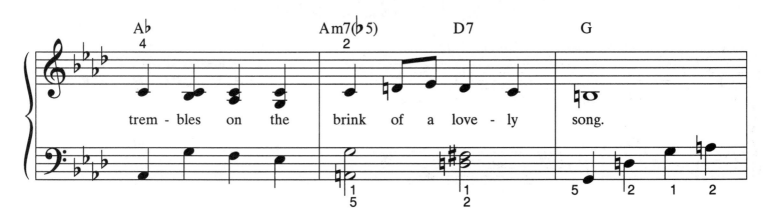

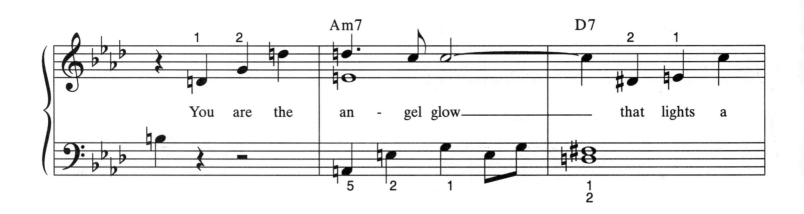

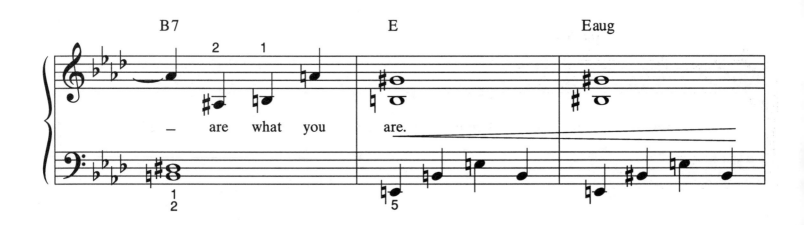

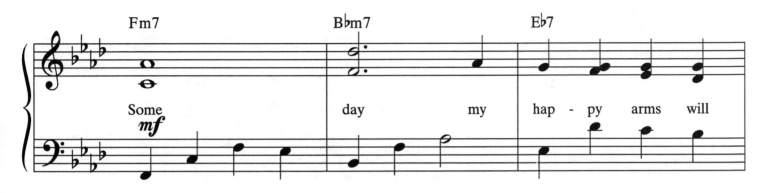

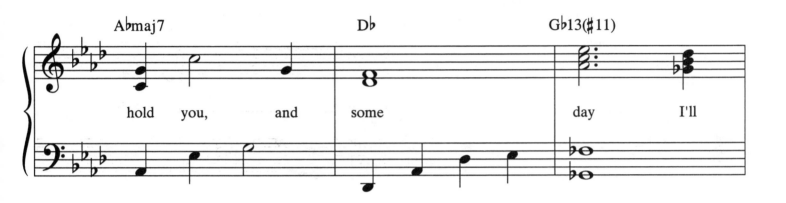

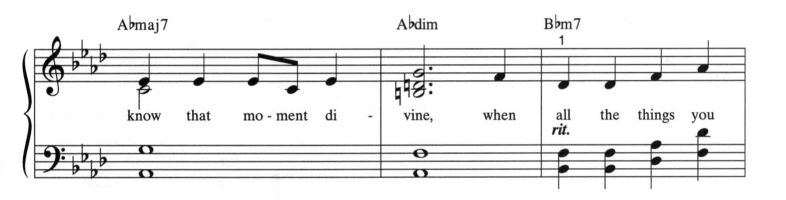

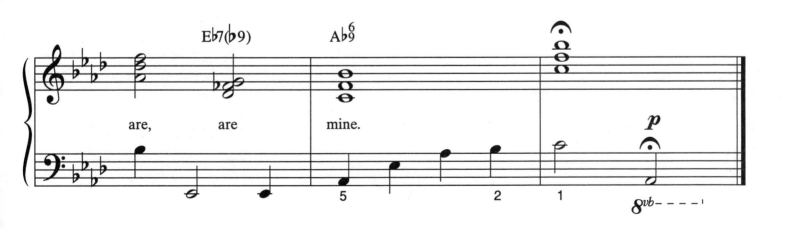

MISTY

The Erroll Garner Trio were the first to record this standard.
Johnny Mathis had the pop hit.

Lyric by JOHNNY BURKE
Music by ERROLL GARNER
Arranged by Richard Bradley

Slowly ♩ = 56

mp Look at me, I'm as help-less as a kit-ten up a tree,_____ and I feel like I'm cling-ing to a cloud; I can't_____ un-der-stand,_____ I get mis-ty just_____ hold-ing your hand.

Walk_____ my

with pedal

Verse 3:
On my own, would I wander through this wonderland alone,
Never knowing my right foot from my left,
My hat from my glove, I'm too misty and too much in love.

WHERE OR WHEN

From the Broadway Musical *Babes in Arms.*

Words by LORENZ HART
Music by RICHARD RODGERS
Arranged by Richard Bradley

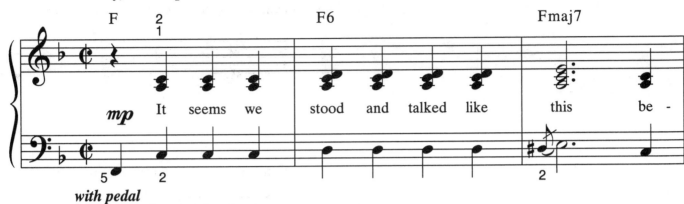

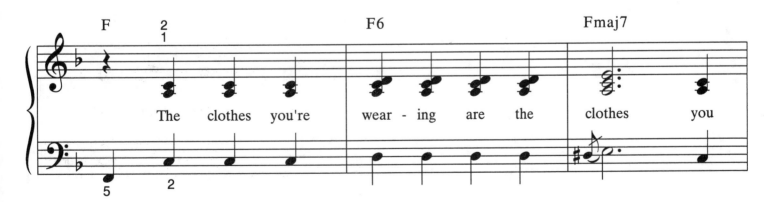

Where or When - 3 - 1

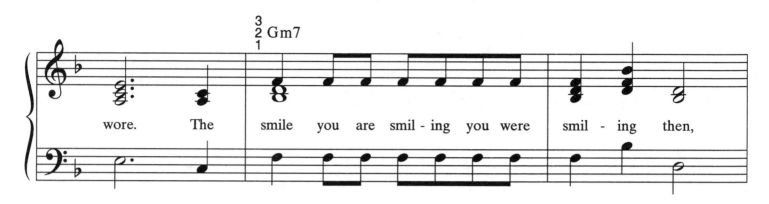

wore. The smile you are smil-ing you were smil-ing then,

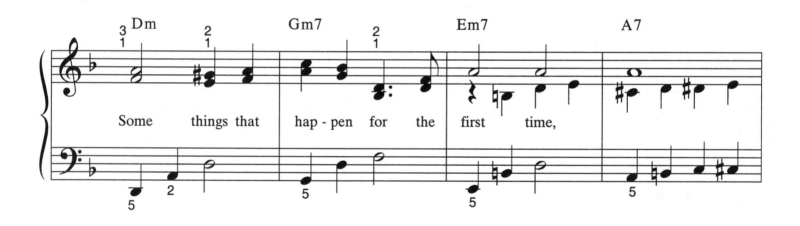

but I can't re-mem-ber where or when.

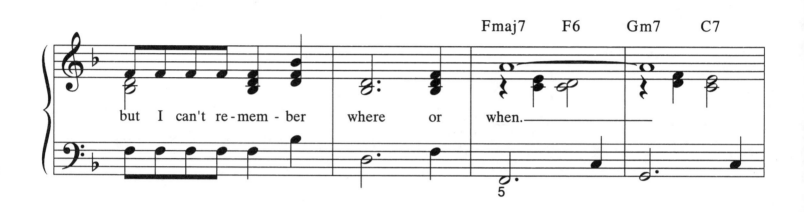

Some things that hap-pen for the first time,

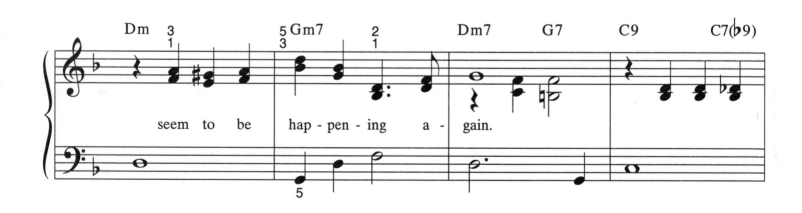

seem to be hap-pen-ing a-gain.

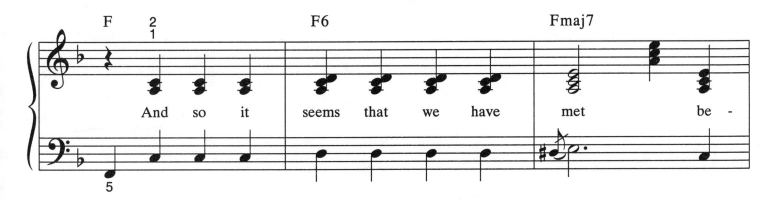

And so it seems that we have met be -

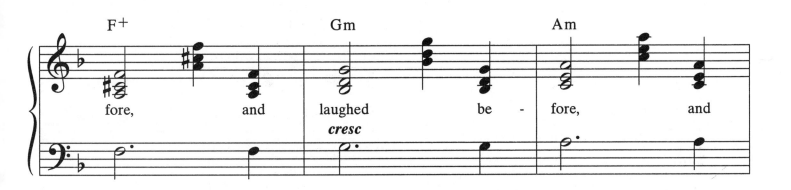

fore, and laughed be - fore, and

cresc

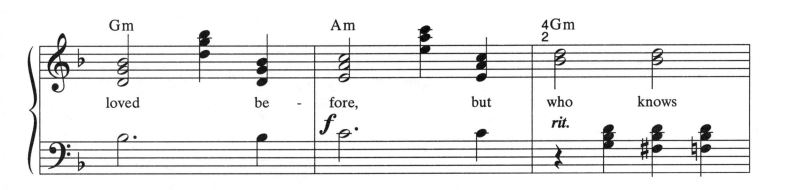

loved be - fore, but who knows

f *rit.*

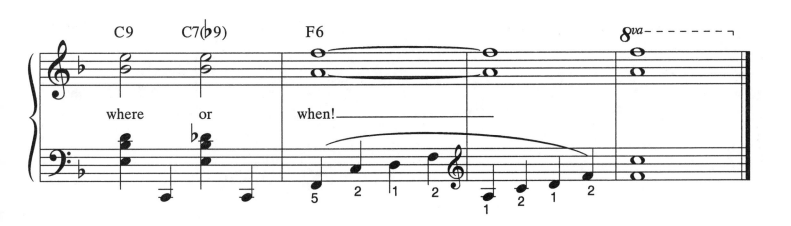

where or when!

SMOKE GETS IN YOUR EYES

From the Broadway Musical *Roberta*

Words by OTTO HARBACH
Music by JEROME KERN
Arranged by Richard Bradley

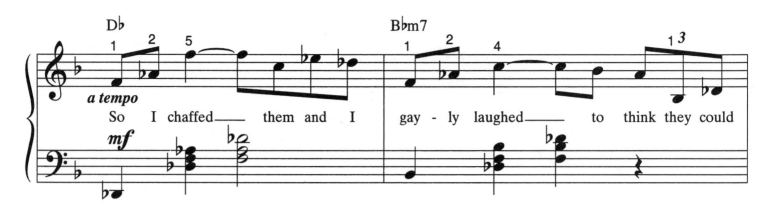

So I chaffed____ them and I gay - ly laughed____ to think they could

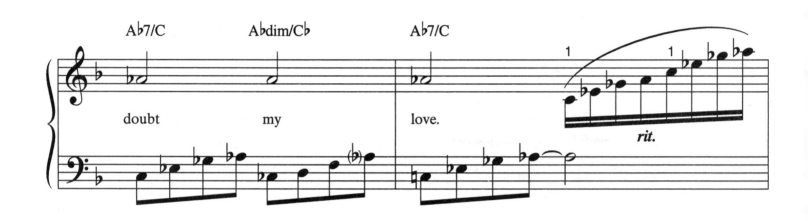

doubt my love.

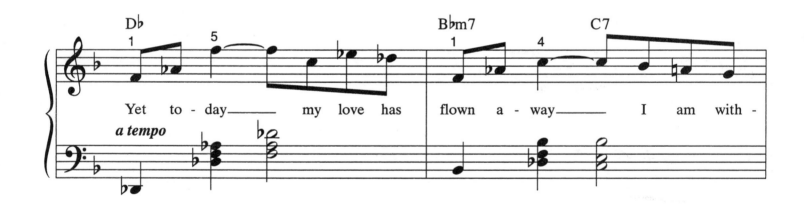

Yet to-day____ my love has flown a - way____ I am with -

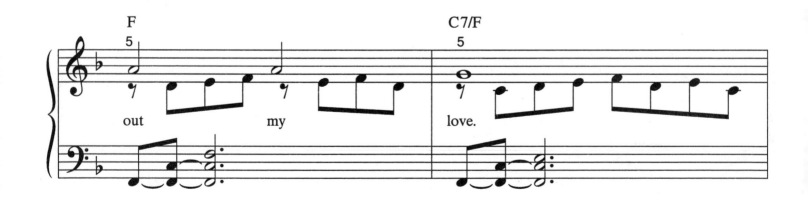

out my love.

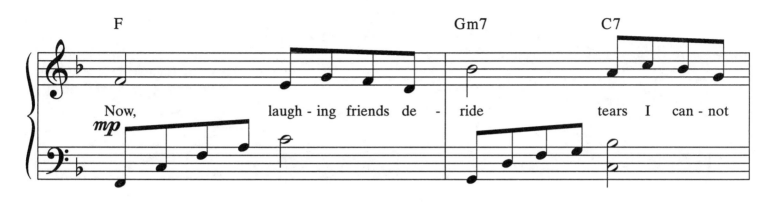

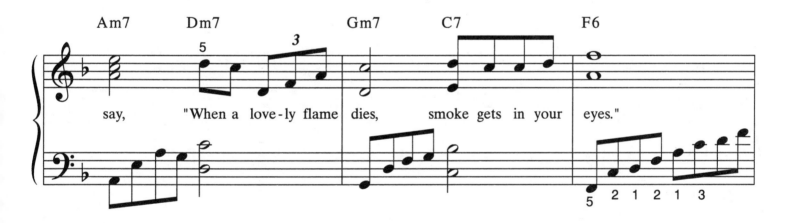

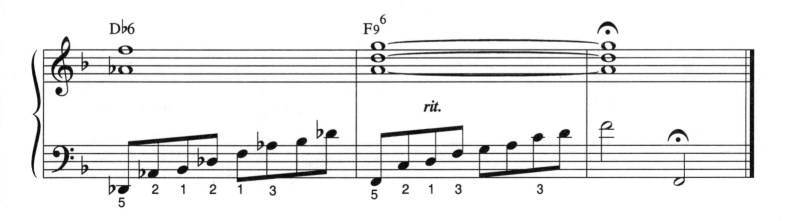

Smoke Gets in Your Eyes - 4 - 4

BEWITCHED
(BOTHERED AND BEWILDERED)

From the Broadway Musical *Pal Joey*

Words by LORENZ HART
Music by RICHARD RODGERS
Arranged by Richard Bradley

Bewitched - 4 - 1

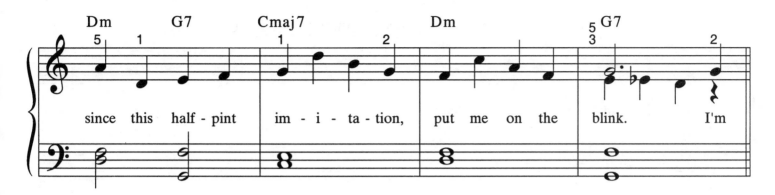

since this half - pint im - i - ta - tion, put me on the blink. I'm

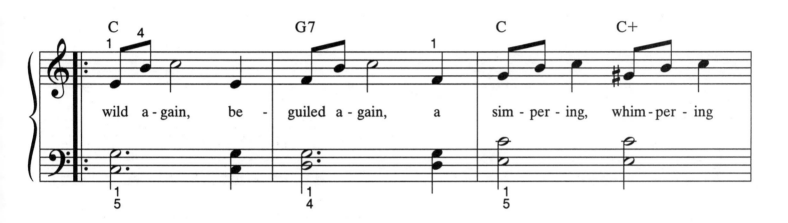

wild a - gain, be - guiled a - gain, a sim - per - ing, whim - per - ing

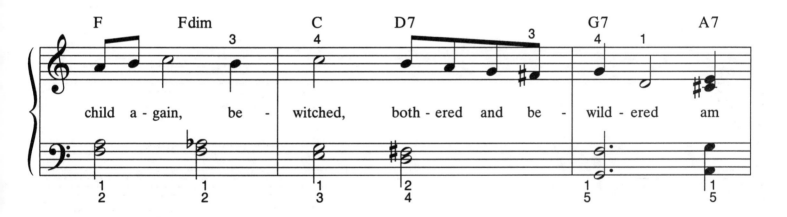

child a - gain, be - witched, both - ered and be - wild - ered am

I. Could-n't sleep, and would-n't sleep, when

love came and told me I shouldn't sleep, be - witched, both-ered and be -

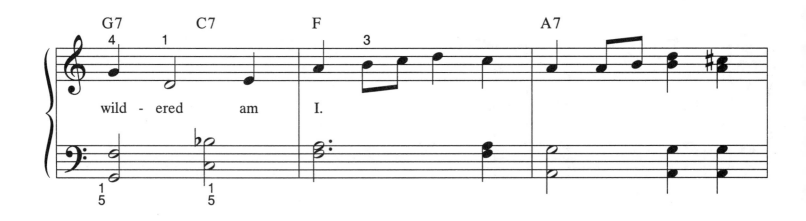

wild - ered am I.

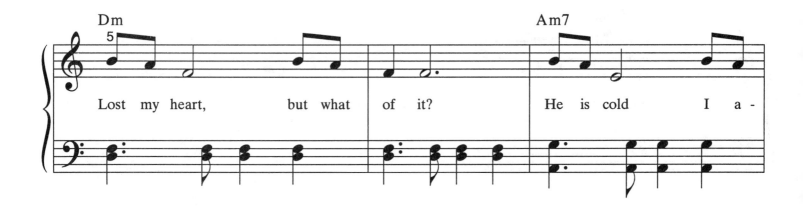

Lost my heart, but what of it? He is cold I a -

gree. He can laugh, but I love it,_____ al-though the

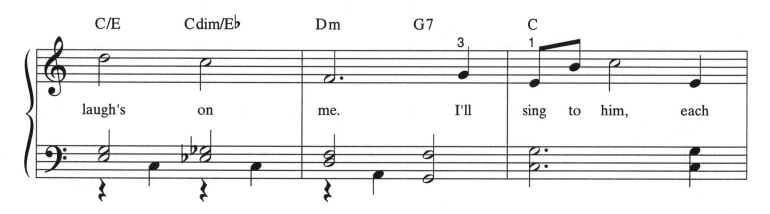

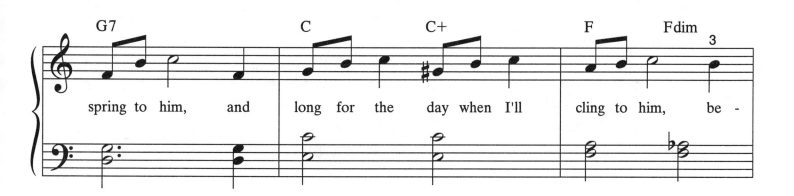

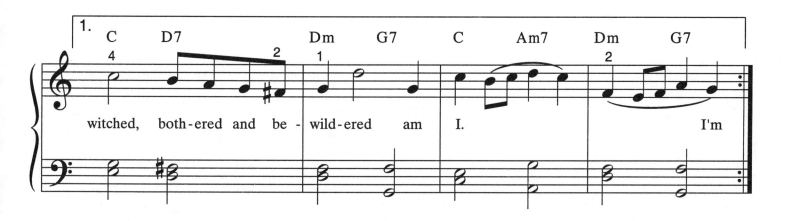

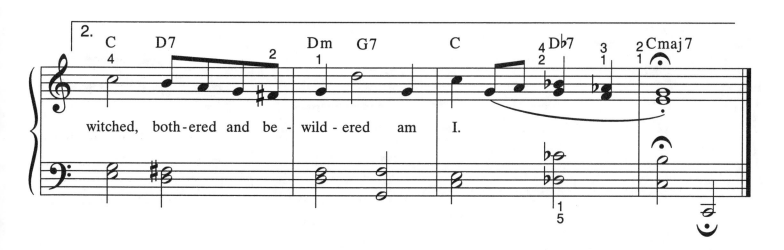

Bewitched - 4 - 4

HEART

From the Broadway Musical *Damn Yankees*

Words and Music by
RICHARD ADLER and JERRY ROSS
Arranged by Richard Bradley

Moderate, with lilt ♩ = 74

Lyrics:
You've got-ta have heart, all you real-ly need is heart, when the odds are say-in' you'll nev-er win,____ that's when the grin____ should start. You've got-ta have hope, must-n't sit a-round and mope,

Heart - 3 - 1

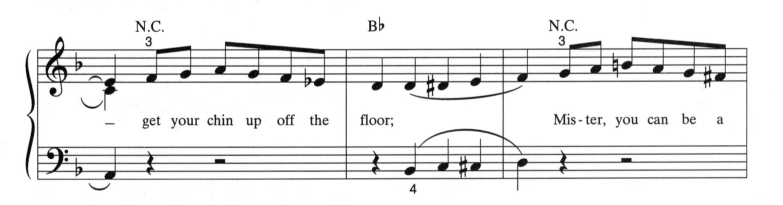

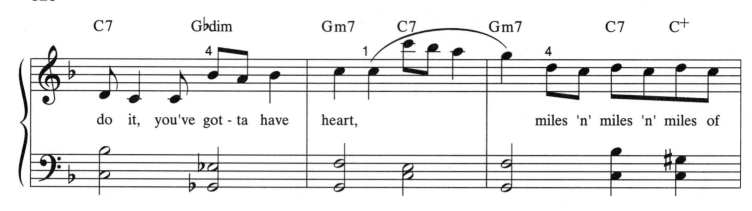

do it, you've got - ta have heart, miles 'n' miles 'n' miles of

heart. Oh, it's fine to be a gen - ius of course,——— but

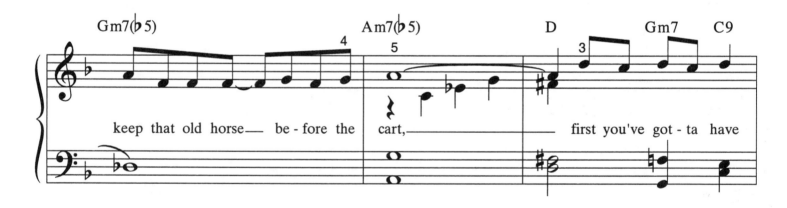

keep that old horse— be - fore the cart,————— first you've got - ta have

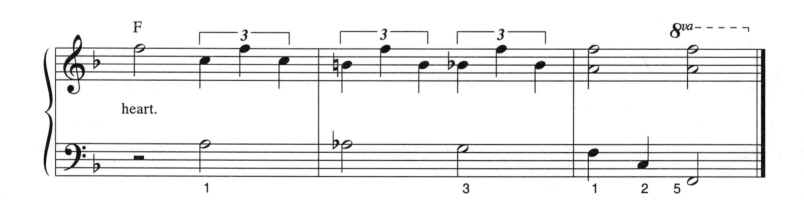

heart.

OL' MAN RIVER

From the Broadway Musical *Show Boat*

Words by OSCAR HAMMERSTEIN II
Music by JEROME KERN
Arranged by Richard Bradley

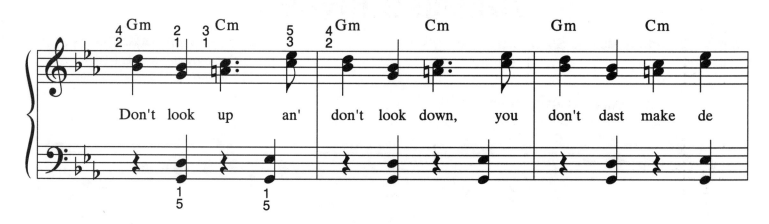

Don't look up an' don't look down, you don't dast make de

white boss frown; Bend yo' knees an' bow yo' head, an'

pull dat rope un - til yo're dead. Let me go 'way from de

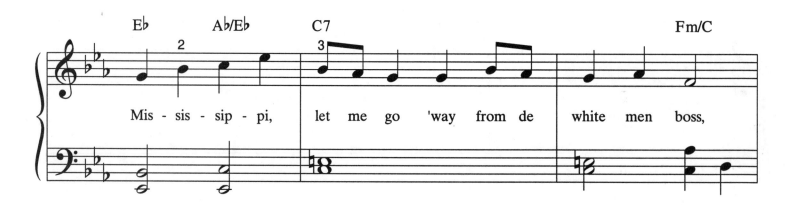

Mis - sis - sip - pi, let me go 'way from de white men boss,

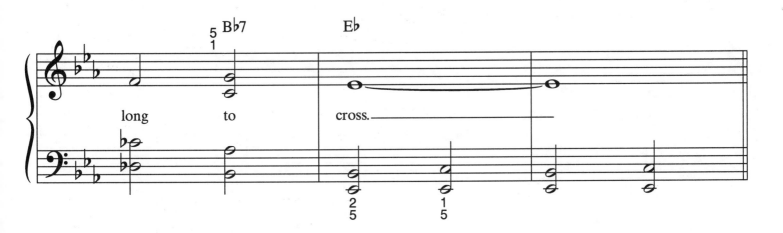

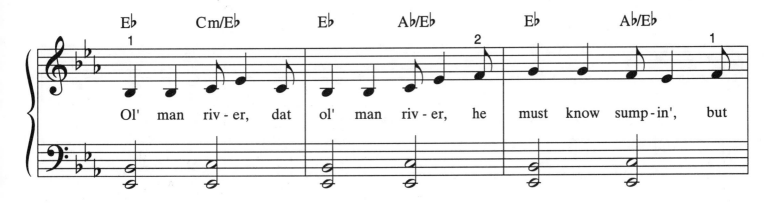

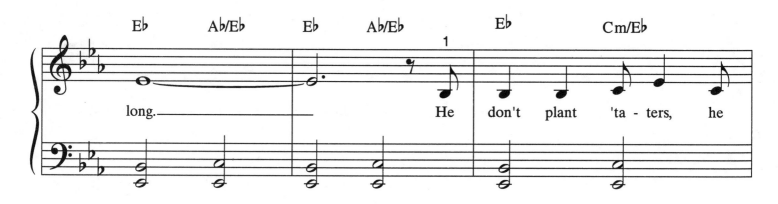

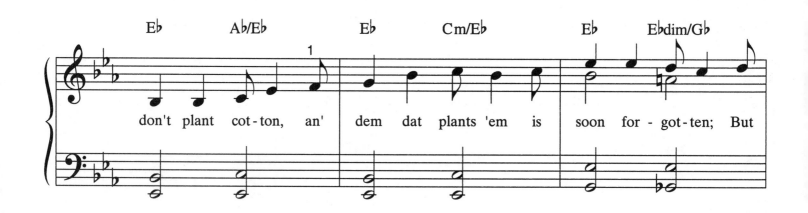

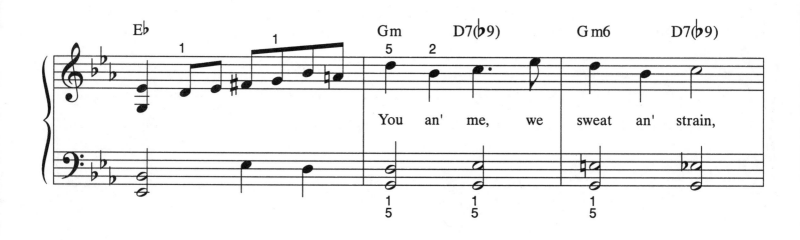

EBB TIDE

Frank Chacksfield & his Orchestra and Stanley Black
& his Orchestra had popular recordings of this standard.

Lyric by CARL SIGMAN
Music by ROBERT MAXWELL
Arranged by Richard Bradley

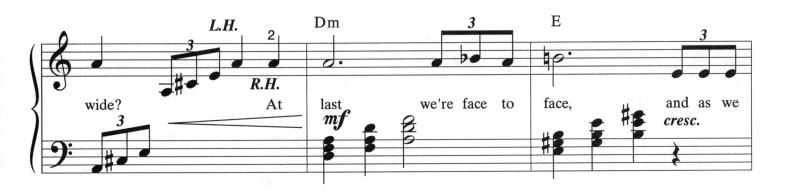

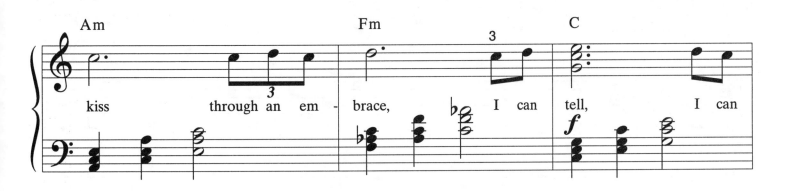

SOMEONE TO WATCH OVER ME

From the Broadway Musical *Oh, Kay!*

Music and Lyrics by
GEORGE GERSHWIN and IRA GERSHWIN
Arranged by Richard Bradley

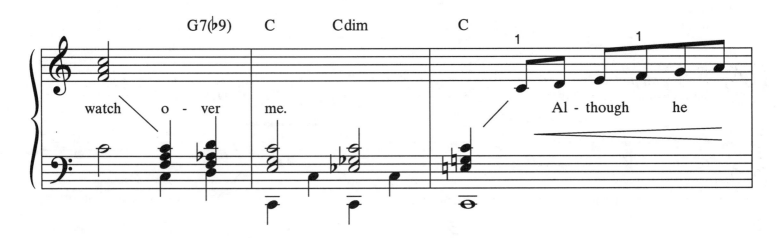

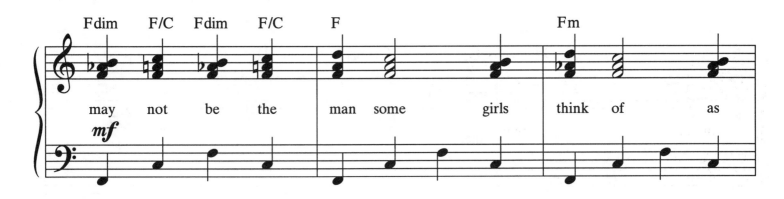

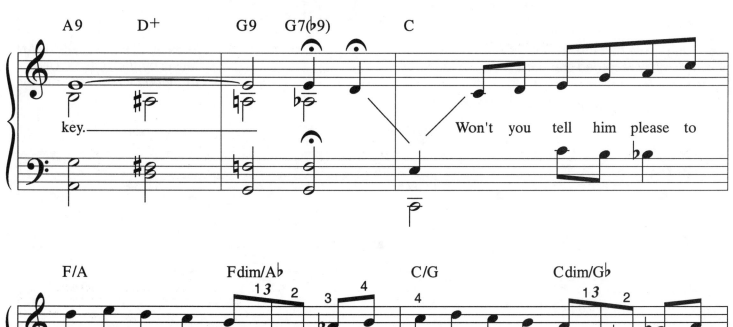

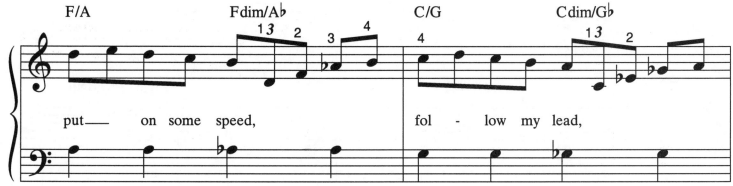

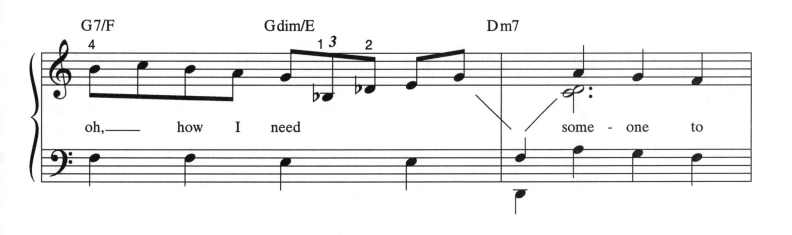

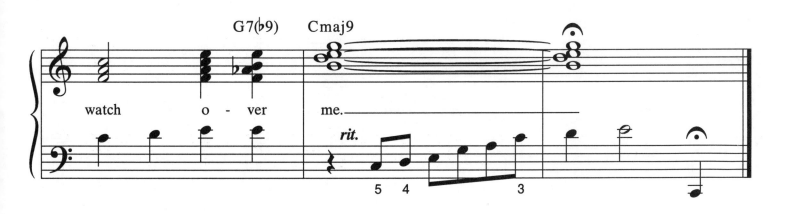

WHEN I FALL IN LOVE

Nat "King" Cole had the first hit with
this frequently recorded standard.

Words by EDWARD HEYMAN
Music by VICTOR YOUNG
Arranged by Richard Bradley

When I Fall in Love - 4 - 1

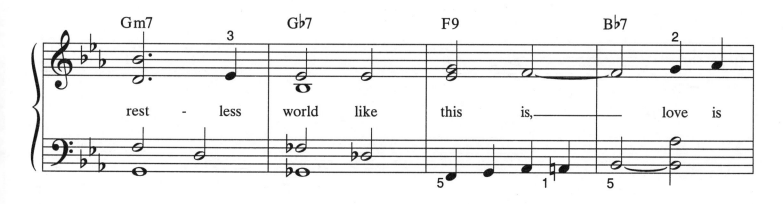

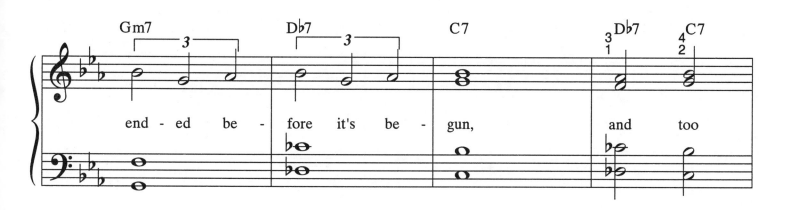

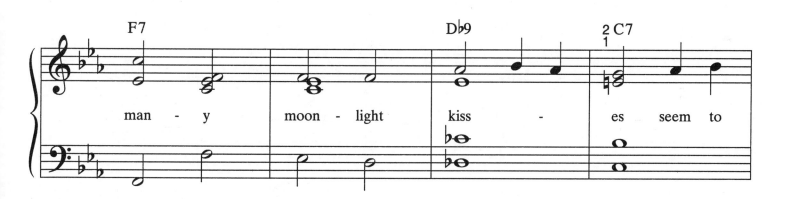

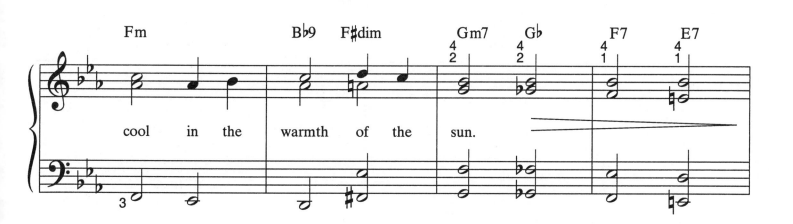

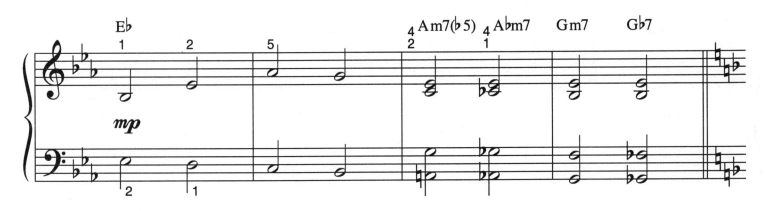

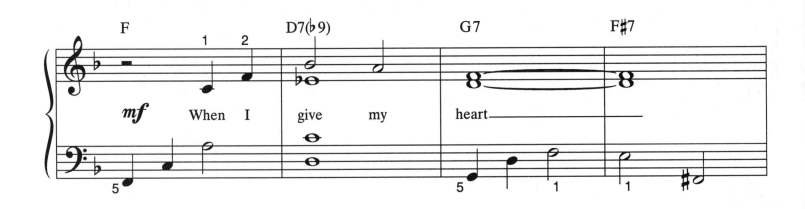

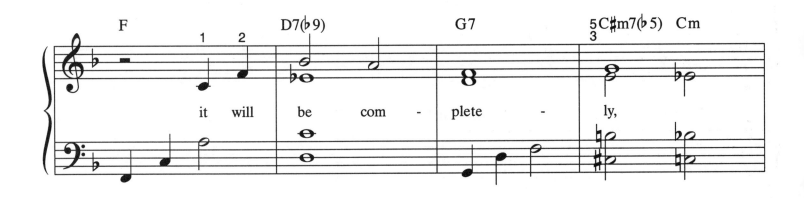

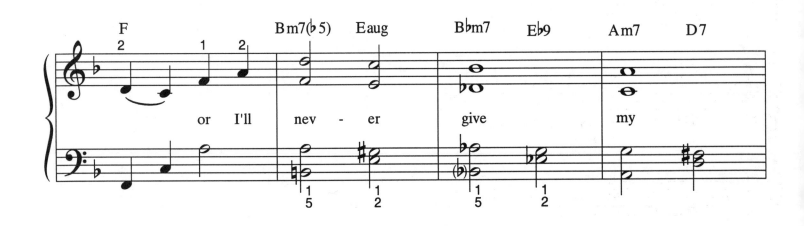

EMBRACEABLE YOU

From the Broadway Musical *Girl Crazy.*

Music and Lyrics by
GEORGE GERSHWIN and IRA GERSHWIN
Arranged by Richard Bradley

Embraceable You - 2 - 1

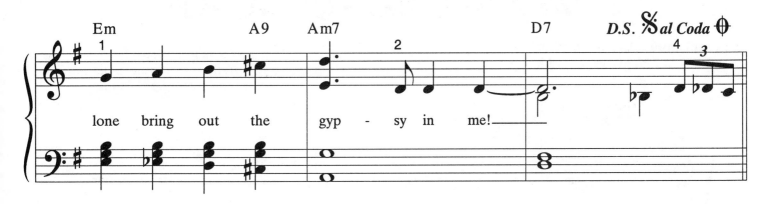

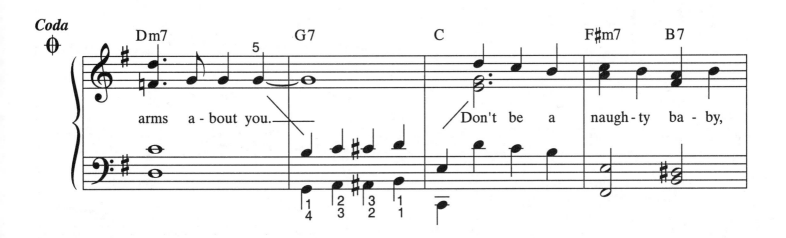

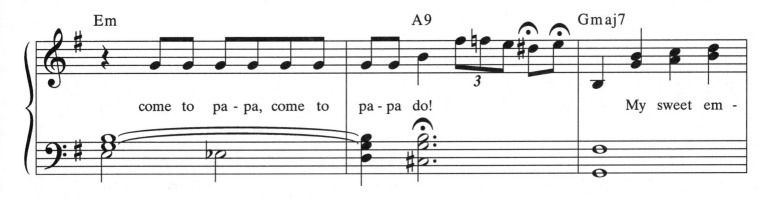

WHAT A WONDERFUL WORLD

Louis Armstrong's recording of this
stanadrd is still frequently heard today.

Words and Music by
GEORGE DAVID WEISS and BOB THIELE
Arranged by Richard Bradley

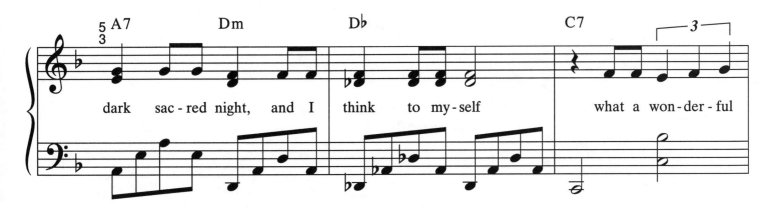

dark sac - red night, and I think to my-self what a won-der-ful

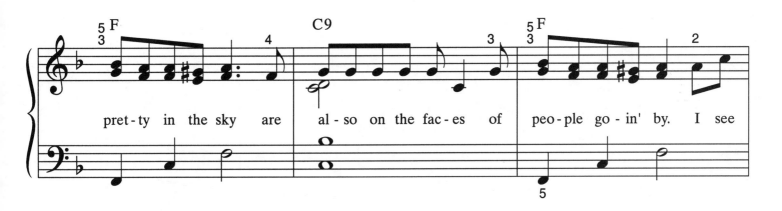

world. The_____ col-ors of the rain-bow, so

pret-ty in the sky are al - so on the fac-es of peo-ple go - in' by. I see

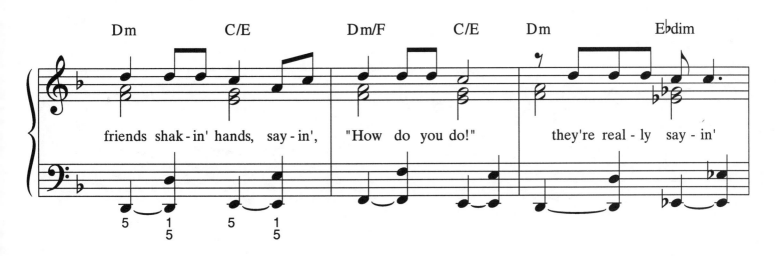

friends shak-in' hands, say-in', "How do you do!" they're real-ly say-in'

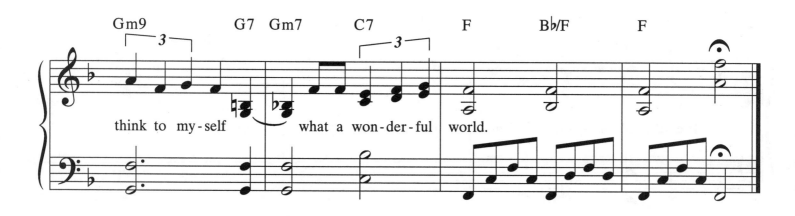

AT LAST

Originally recorded by Glenn Miller & his Orchestra,
At Last is sung by Etta James on the soundtrack of
the motion picture *Living Out Loud*.

Lyric by MACK GORDON
Music by HARRY WARREN
Arranged by Richard Bradley

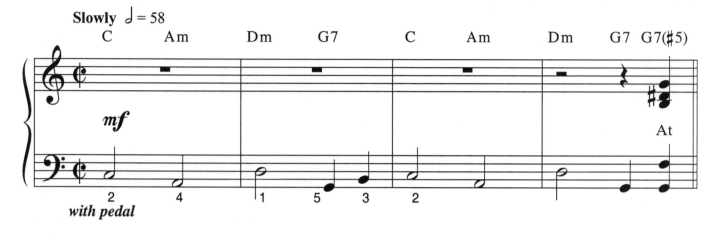

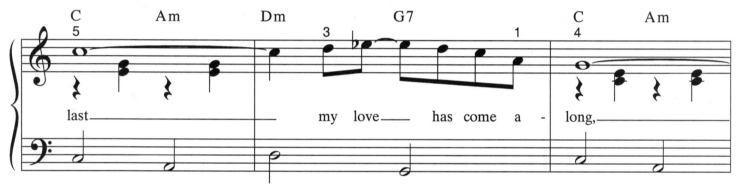

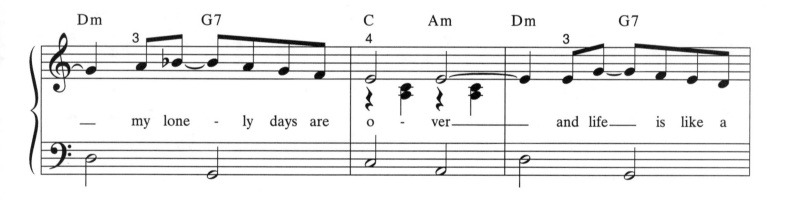

At Last - 3 - 1

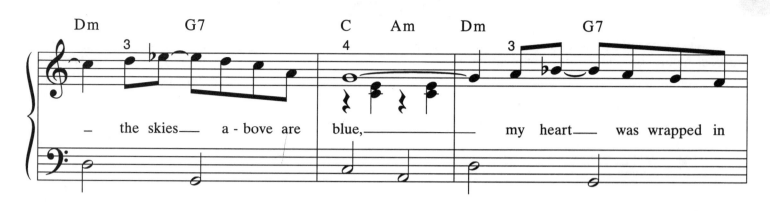

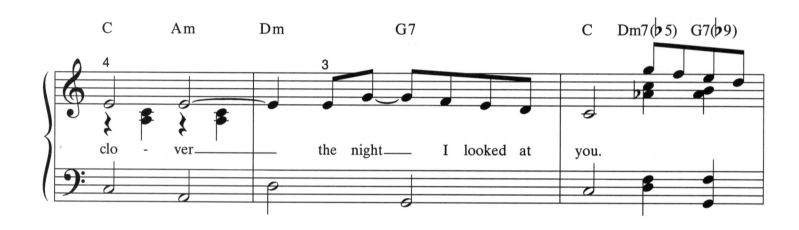

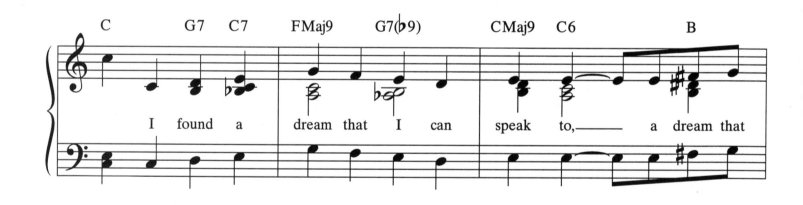

cheek to,   a   thrill I've nev - er   known.   You

smiled_____   and then_____ the spell was   cast_____

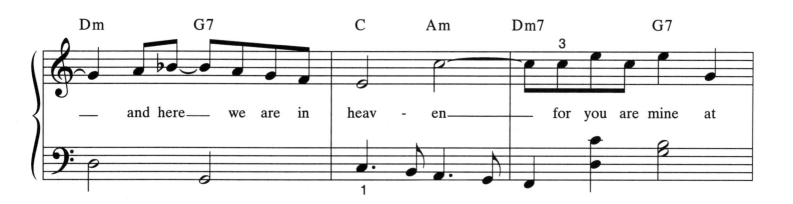

___ and here___ we are in   heav - en_____ for you are mine at

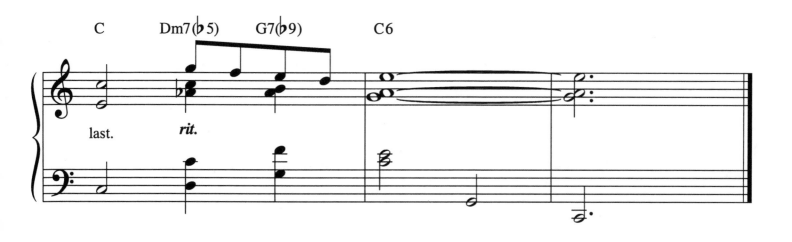

last.   *rit.*

MY FUNNY VALENTINE

This standard from the Broadway Musical *Babes in Arms* was also featured in the film *Pal Joey*.

Words by LORENZ HART
Music by RICHARD RODGERS
Arranged by Richard Bradley

Slowly, with expression ♩ = 94

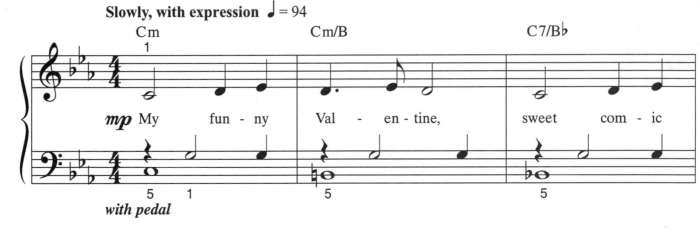

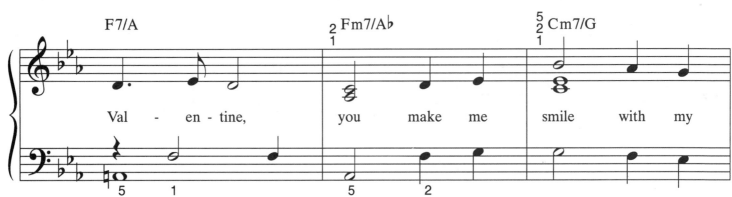

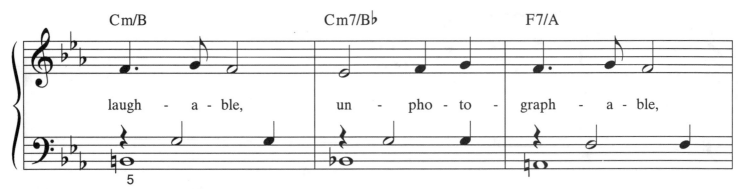

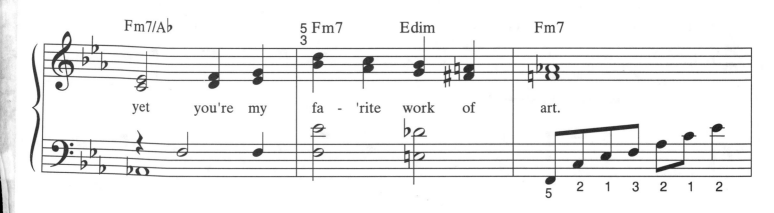

yet   you're   my   fa - 'rite work   of   art.

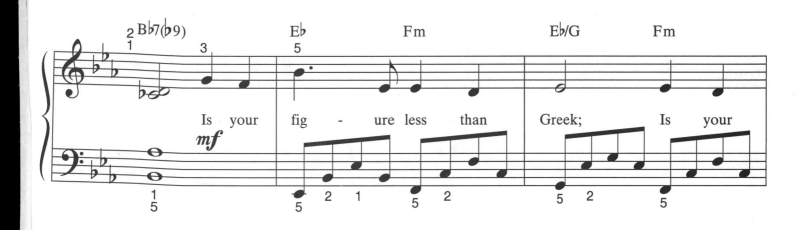

Is   your   fig - ure less   than   Greek;   Is   your

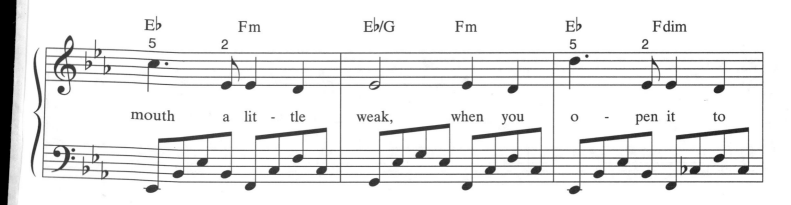

mouth   a lit - tle   weak,   when you   o - pen it to

speak,   are you   smart?

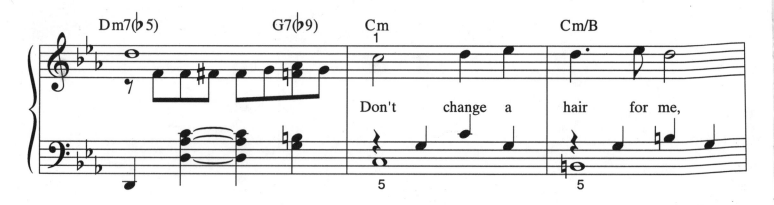

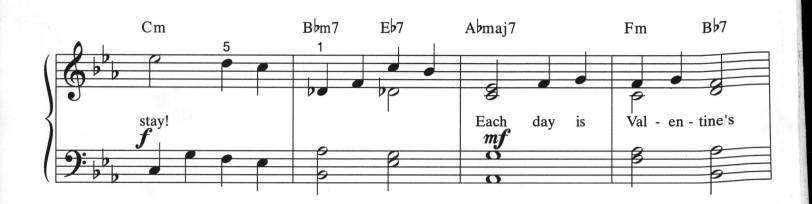

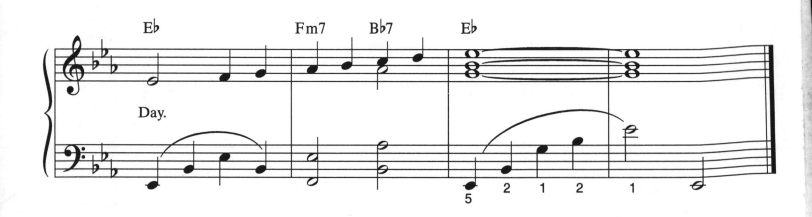